NO QUICK FIX

Healing the Fractured Family

WORLD IMPACT
2001 S. Vermont Ave.
Los Angeles, CA 90007

Foreword by Pat Boone
KEITH PHILLIPS

A Division of GL Publications
Ventura, California, U.S.A.

This book is dedicated to all my co-laborers who contributed to and prayed for its completion, especially Mary Thiessen, Susie Krehbiel and Arletta Henry who labored with me above and beyond the call of duty and learned afresh that in writing a book there is no quick fix.

Rights for publishing this book in other languages are contracted by Gospel Literature International foundation (GLINT). GLINT also provides technical help for the adaptation, translation, and publishing of Bible study resources and books in more than 100 languages worldwide. For further information, contact GLINT, Post Office Box 6688, Ventura, California 93006, U.S.A., or the publisher.

Except where otherwise indicated, Scripture quotations are from:
Holy Bible: *The New International Version.* Copyright © 1978 by The International Bible Society. Used by permission of Zondervan Bible Publishers.
Also quoted is the *KJV—Authorized King James Version.*

The characters, settings and events in this narrative are true. To protect the privacy of the individual, fictitious names are often used.

8-88

Published by Regal Books
A Division of GL Publications
Ventura, California 93006
Printed in U.S.A.

Library of Congress Cataloging in Publication Data

Phillips, Keith W.
   No quick fix.

    1. Church work with families—United States.
2. Family—United States—Religious life. 3. Slums—
United States. I. Title.
BV4438.P45   1985   261.8'3585   85-10879
ISBN 0-8307-1078-7
ISBN 0-8307-1077-9 (pbk.)

CONTENTS

FOREWORD

I'm not very comfortable when I think about America's ghettos. The filth, poverty and violence almost make me turn away.

But I can't do that. Christ would not have done that. Instead of turning away, our Lord went right in and ministered to the poor, touched the lepers, healed the sick and freed the oppressed. Wherever He walked, despair was turned to hope.

Today Christ is walking through the garbage-strewn streets of the ghetto. Over 100 missionaries—single men and women, couples and whole families with children—have moved right into the poorest, most dangerous communities in our country to minister with World Impact.

They bring love to the neglected children of our cities, comfort to the victims of senseless violence and hope to those trapped in degrading poverty.

It all began 20 years ago when my friend, Dr. Keith Phillips, first walked into a housing project in Watts. This young minister taught the good news of Jesus Christ and cared for the obvious physical needs of his new friends. He brought them food, clothes and shoes—and most of all, God's love.

For two decades, Keith and his fellow World Impact workers have been living and teaching the love of Christ in the ghettos of America. Because they live in the ghetto, side by side with the people they help, they are there when an emergency arises and when tragedy strikes. And through them, Christ lives in the inner city.

No Quick Fix shares the exciting miracles God is performing in urban America. It's painfully honest about the setbacks that also occur. Here is a realistic approach to replacing the brokenness in our inner cities with the wholeness of Christ.

I wholeheartedly recommend *No Quick Fix* because I've been in the ghetto. I filmed *The Cross and the Switchblade* in Fort Greene in the Bronx, and in Harlem. I felt the suffocating poverty, the hunger, the fear, the despair. And I thought if there were no hope for these dear people, I would not be able to handle it. But friend, there is hope.

This book is the new *Cross and the Switchblade,* with its electrifying mix of desperate problems and miraculous answers, human degradation and divine love, violence and tenderness, deadend streets and newly opening doors.

No Quick Fix documents that Jesus of Nazareth is still walking among the poor—that He is *their* Prophet, Priest and King. And because of the tangible, visible love of Christ in the ghetto, they have a solid hope and a bright future.

Read this book prayerfully. And then rejoice because our God says, "For I know the plans I have for you . . . plans to prosper you and not to harm you, plans to give you hope and a future" (Jer. 29:11).

Pat Boone
Beverly Hills, California

PREFACE

Rather naively I walked into our worship service expecting to preach a well-prepared sermon, greet those in attendance and leave for a delicious dinner.

I should have known better.

Scorpion, a well-groomed, articulate young man, smiled warmly as he shook my hand. Scorpion had been a big-time drug dealer and one of the most feared dudes on the street. He carried a .357 magnum. He always collected the money owed him.

No one messed with Scorpion. He almost killed one man with a poker iron, but was out of jail within a day. No charges were pressed.

A few months earlier one of our missionaries had led 26-year-old Scorpion to Christ. The change was remarkable. Scorpion flushed his drugs down the toilet, cut off relationships with his old friends and moved back into his mother's home.

But Scorpion had a problem. Shortly before he had become a Christian he'd had two different girlfriends. Now both of these women were expecting his child. And both of them had become Christians.

Scorpion's question was simple: "Which one should I marry?"

Never in my 20 years of ministry in the inner city had I been confronted with a more puzzling spiritual dilemma. It would have taxed the wisdom of Solomon.

I used to know all the answers.

If a person was lonely, anxious or troubled he needed to accept Christ as his Saviour. If a person was depressed, confused or hurting he needed to claim God's forgiveness and enjoy His peace.

The Bible remains true. But sin has so perverted man that Scripture does not directly address many modern aberrations of God's law.

What would you say to 45-year-old Shirley who has four children by four different men? As a new Christian, she wants to know to which man she should reconcile.

What would you say to 16-year-old Angie who does not understand how she can submit to her parents? Her father has raped her for years and continues to want her to sleep with him.

What would you say to 12-year-old Luis, whose father forces him to smuggle drugs across the border? His dad says he will kill Luis if he refuses to cooperate.

What would you say to seven-year-old Jimmy whose older brother taught him how to steal food? Jimmy explains, "We search through garbage cans, try to earn money and even beg for food. But when we get real hungry, we steal. Will God send me to hell for that?"

One could become perplexed, discouraged and even tempted to write off the ghetto. But Jesus would not do that and neither can we. Christ has passed on to Christians His baton of bringing the gospel, reconciliation and freedom to the oppressed.

There is no easy answer. There is no quick fix.

SECTION ONE
THE FAMILY: GOD'S INSTITUTION

"For I have chosen him, so that he will direct his children and his household after him to keep the way of the Lord by doing what is right and just."

Genesis 18:19

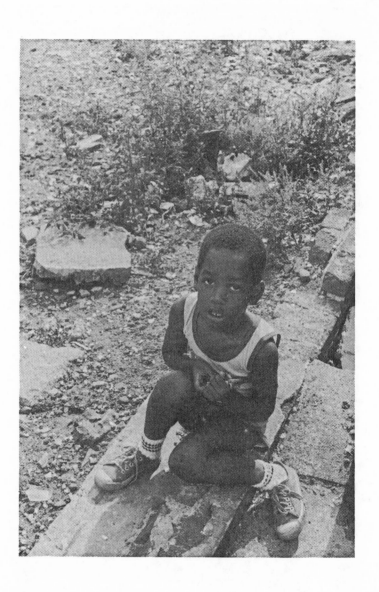

1

BROKEN HOMES AND FRACTURED FAMILIES

The impoverishment of the ghetto is often measured by the escalating crime rate, malnutrition, illiteracy, unemployment and addiction. But the greatest crisis—the root of all these problems—is the fractured family.

We have no doubt that Satan is plotting to render a death blow to the human race by focusing his energy on destroying the family unit. Jerome's life illustrates how devastated a child without a family can be.

THE CYCLE BEGINS:
A Child Without a Family

Eighteen-year-old Jerome is trapped in the body and mind of a child. He does not appear to be a day over 12. I had heard that childhood neglect and abuse could thwart a person's physical and mental development. Apparently, that happened to Jerome.

Jerome is a misfit. He hates himself and cannot understand "why my mother kept my brother, but not me." Yet even before Jerome's mother abandoned him the seeds of tragedy were sown.

Jerome's earliest years were saturated with neglect. He has no memory of his mother playing with him. She virtually ignored him. When he got up in the morning he had to dress himself and get out of the house before he got whipped for making a mistake. She never fixed breakfast for him and seldom said good-bye to him when he went out.

Once Jerome got outside he begged for money to buy candy. It was a good way to kill time until classes started. The free lunch at school was the one sure meal he had on weekdays. On Saturdays and Sundays he had to scrounge for whatever food he could find.

After school Jerome usually went home with a friend. He tried to hang around long enough to eat supper there. He rarely returned to his own house until after 9:00 P.M. Then he went straight to bed.

Jerome grew up plagued by fear. Street gangs shot and stabbed people outside his house. Addicts and drunks were everywhere. One day Jerome watched the coroner take away the body of his neighbor who had been brutally murdered. "I hope it don't happen to me!" he cried.

It was not much safer inside Jerome's home. Time after time thieves broke in. The police simply said, "Someday the people who robbed you will get robbed too." Small consolation for a child.

Jerome never liked elementary school. He was depressed by the guards and heavy chains on the doors. He carried a knife to protect himself from older boys who tried to steal his free lunch.

Jerome lived in five different foster homes in four

years. He was beaten severely and regularly. He spent months at the County Children's Shelter. He knew he was unwanted.

Jerome protected himself from his hostile environment through lying. He lied so much he became unable to distinguish between fact and illusion. He waivered between angry outbursts and wild fantasies.

Jerome's peers picked on him and teased him because he was so small for his age. Even though it hurt, Jerome got used to their physical attacks and verbal ridicule.

But Jerome never accepted his mother's rejection.

One day Jerome's mother called the foster home to say that Jerome could come back to live with her. He packed all his earthly belongings in a sack and set out for this much-anticipated reconciliation with his real mom and his brother. Jerome's mind raced with happy thoughts. He could just imagine a big smile and a warm hug from his own mom. He couldn't wait to be part of a family again.

When Jerome got to his mother's place he flew up the stairs and eagerly knocked on the door. As the door opened his smile broadened.

And then it happened—that long-awaited reunion.

"What you want, boy?" Jerome's mother barked.

Jerome tried to remind her that she had invited him to live with her. "Maybe I did. I was probably drunk. Anyway, I ain't got no time for you. You got a place now," she scowled. "Get out of here."

"Can a mother forget the baby at her breast and have no compassion on the child she has borne?" (Isa. 49:15).

Jerome never went to high school. He could not keep up academically or emotionally. Instead he turned to the drug dealers who infested his neighborhood. They "used" Jerome to deliver their dope. Jerome wanted friends and approval so badly he did whatever the junkies told him. He stole from his foster mother for them, he lied for them— all to earn their friendship.

The addicts repaid Jerome by constantly making him the butt of their jokes, and their scapegoat when caught by the police. Jerome never understood that he was being used even though the rest of the neighborhood did.

After attending our teen-age Bible club for several months Jerome openly expressed his faith in Christ. He loved our staff, listened attentively to the Bible lessons and promised to do whatever we asked. Yet in spite of his good intentions, Jerome seldom followed through. And because of his deep problems I wondered how much we could truly help him.

When Jerome turned 18 he was thrown out onto the streets—too old for foster care, too immature to fend for himself. He had no education, no job, no hope. We found him sleeping in an abandoned, burned-out building in the dead of winter.

We Had to Do Something!

I decided that we would send Jerome to our Christian Leadership Training Center located on a 560-acre ranch in Kansas. Jerome did not qualify for the program, but I felt we could help restore his dignity by providing projects which he could undertake and accomplish. Our staff would love him without restraint. If they couldn't help him, I knew of no people who could.

Jerome's first day in Kansas dramatically revealed that we had underestimated his severe deprivation. Al Ewert, our Midwest Vice-President, picked Jerome up at the bus depot.

Before Al took Jerome to the Training Center they dropped by our women's staff home in Wichita. When Al pulled into the driveway Jerome became ecstatic. He mistook the small house with its green lawn for the ranch.

Then Al bought Jerome a hamburger, fries and a Coke. The hamburger and Coke were gone in a flash, but Jerome methodically slipped the fries into his pocket. Al had to promise Jerome that he would eat again that day before he was able to enjoy his fries.

On the way to our ranch Jerome's face was plastered to the window. He thought the grain elevators in a small town were skyscrapers, like in New York. They passed acres of corn. Jerome could not believe that Al was being straight with him about corn growing on those large plants. Jerome just "knew" corn came in a can.

When Jerome actually arrived at the ranch he was overwhelmed at its size. He beamed when he saw the nice house in which he would live. He was delighted with the animals and politely said "hi" to each calf as he patted it on the head. He was awestruck when one calf sucked on his finger. Jerome knew that the calf was trying to tell him, "I really like you."

Jerome was fascinated by the chickens until it registered that he had eaten some of their kin at "the Colonel's." Even more startling, he suddenly realized where eggs came from.

Jerome spent his first day digging a trench. When he finished he glowed with pride. That weekend he landed the biggest catfish ever caught at the ranch.

It Still Hurts!

But within a week Jerome's severe problems surfaced. When we asked him about a fence he'd been assigned to paint, Jerome said that he had already done it. However, he had not even started.

When we asked Jerome to gather eggs, he assured us that he had completed that chore. Then we took him to the hen house and directed his attention to the ungathered eggs. "Boy, these chickens sure lay those things fast," he remarked.

Jerome lived in a fantasy world. He claimed to have trained the Newark police force how to shoot weapons. He vividly described how he had shot a fox with a bow and arrow on Central Avenue in Newark. He boasted that he had built homes and had owned sports cars.

And once Jerome said something, he would never back down. Whenever we attempted to reason with him, he'd want to fight. And he tried to fight a lot.

Jim Elam, a staff member at our Training Center, is a powerful, former college football player with a kind heart and gentle manner. When Jim pointed out something Jerome should have done, Jerome exploded. He tried to physically throw Jim out of the room even though Jim was more than twice Jerome's weight. I am sure it took a lot of self-control for Jim not to put Jerome in his place. Jim could just imagine the story the next day about how Jerome had "whipped" him.

Unfortunately Jerome's lying and his violent outbursts forced us to send him back to the city. We loved him and wished he could have stayed, but we also understood that, in the best interests of the other young men at the Training Center, Jerome could no longer remain.

Taking Jerome back to the Wichita bus depot was painful. He did not say a word as we drove off the property. Huge tears poured from his eyes as he looked for the last time at the ranch. It was probably the only home he had ever had.

Jerome had gained close to 20 pounds in the few weeks he had stayed with us. He'd had three meals a day, his own bed, warm clothes and people who loved him. I felt cruel sending him away, but we had no other option. It still hurts to think about him.

If only we had found Jerome sooner—before the severe beatings, the loneliness, the rejection—before his wounds were so deep. All we can do now is be available to love Jerome without restriction and pray that God will perform a miracle of healing in body, mind and soul.

Jerome's family situation is not unique. Countless times parents' sins impact negatively upon their children.

And the tragedy of the broken family—the rejection, abuse and immorality—grows geometrically with each generation.

THE CYCLE REPEATS:
40 Years Later

In many ways, Bea is just like Jerome. Bea also came from a broken home with multiple fathers. She too grew up feeling rejected and unloved by her mother. But Bea is 40 years older than Jerome. And her longer life vividly illustrates the proliferation of the broken family in each succeeding generation.

Bea had her first of 12 children when she was 14. Her husband, a heroin addict, was constantly in and out of jail. While he was incarcerated, Bea went out with other men. Then when Bea's husband came home he would brutally beat her and the children. Finally, he deserted them.

Bea's children and grandchildren are now copying her life-style.

Bea's 21-year-old daughter Patrice is the mother of two children, but she acts as though her youngsters do not exist. Patrice runs around with young teenagers. Her boyfriend is only 15. She does not want her friends to know that she has kids, so she often locks them in the house alone—no lights, no food, no love. Bea fears that her grandchildren will be killed if there is a fire, but Patrice will not give her mother a key to their apartment.

When Patrice is home, she whips her two boys with hangers and extension cords. She slaps their faces so hard you can see her handprint hours later. Patrice explains her surprise at what some people call child abuse: "Some kids just tear up easier than others."

Patrice often makes four-year-old Wayne stay in bed all day without toys. Wayne suffers from severe malnutrition. He is very small except for his bloated stomach.

Wayne lives in constant terror of his absentee father, who brutally beats Wayne to get back at Patrice. His tiny body is covered with bruises and welts.

Every time Wayne attends Bible club, he remembers his Scripture verse and is excited to learn about God. When Bea saw Wayne happily singing at a Bible club program, she said, "I've never seen him smile before." Bible club is the one bright spot in Wayne's existence.

Unfortunately, Wayne often cannot come to Bible club because Patrice says he is sleeping or is not dressed. We encourage Patrice to dress him and assure her we will wait for him. How we want to rescue him out of that place.

The insidious cycle has come full circle: Bea's mother—Bea—Patrice—Wayne. Bea's family represents four generations of hurt, heartbreak and hopelessness. And unless there is divine intervention this domestic destruction will repeat itself ad infinitum.

Children like Jerome and mothers like Bea represent a great unanswered problem in urban America: the fractured family. The government, social agencies and the Church have been equally negligent in failing to provide a realistic response.

2

THE WAGES OF SIN . . .

God ordained the family unit as the basic building block of society. He commissioned parents to love and be faithful to each other. This preserves purity, morality and social order. It also provides "living models" after which the children can pattern their lives. When God's plan is ignored, the consequences are awesome.

The mother and father are seriously scarred when a family crumbles. But the children pay the biggest price. They are not only the immediate victims, but they will probably perpetuate the same home life for their offspring unless someone breaks this vicious cycle.

The lives of our Bible club children demonstrate the tragic results of their parents' sin.

NEGLECT

Solomon, 5, often played alone on the third floor of an empty tenement. His young, unmarried mother was too busy growing up herself to care for him.

Solomon didn't seem to mind. He was in heaven rummaging through the debris and rubble. The broken plaster was perfect cargo for his treasured dump truck. And besides, it was quiet—unlike his overcrowded apartment. He seldom saw anyone in this gutted building, except for drunks. And they were usually asleep.

One afternoon Solomon was off in his usual dreamworld, studiously transporting plaster from one "dump" to another. Halfway through one trip, he thought he heard someone in the room. As he turned to look, two older boys grabbed his truck and deliberately shoved him out the window. Solomon screamed, but could not prevent the disastrous 30-foot fall.

Solomon told us, "When the police arrived they breathed into my mouth 'cause my heart stopped ticking. They didn't have time to wait for an ambulance, so they took me to the hospital in their squad car. They took the two guys to a home for bad boys—and I got a plate put in my head."

The ghetto is a treacherous place for unsupervised children. Yet it is common for unattended youngsters to play on the busy streets or to explore half-gutted tenements.

The jagged scar jetting across Solomon's forehead and the lumpy crevices covering his skull bear solemn testimony that many young mothers believe it is acceptable to ignore their children. These parents "can't be bothered" with playing with their kids or following them around.

Some neglect, however, is more blatant—outright criminal.

The mother of five-year-old Henry has given birth to

21 children: 13 live with her, four were killed in a terrible fire in their previous apartment and the others run the streets.

Life's troubles seem to have been too much for Henry's distraught mother. She leaves her youngest children alone in their half-burned-out apartment while she drinks and plays cards on the street corner with other jobless men and women. The little comfort she finds is dearly paid for by her neglected youngsters.

One afternoon Henry left his tiny apartment and cautiously walked by the vagrants and addicts who lined the hallway. How he hated the stench of human waste and rotting garbage. He could hardly wait to get outside.

Henry bounced his ball on the glass-covered sidewalk. When it rolled into the busy street he darted after it and was struck by a car. Both of his legs were broken.

After spending months in the hospital Henry came home in a body cast. He could move nothing but his head and his arms. He could neither roll over nor sit up by himself.

That would be torture enough for any little boy. But Henry's plight was much more heartbreaking. His mother continued to sit on the street corner apparently undaunted by the pain of her own flesh and blood.

I couldn't believe it. When my five-year-old, David, scratches his arm or stubs his toe I hurt with him. How could any parent not want to love and comfort her suffering child? Henry's mother's indifference was beyond my comprehension.

Martha, Henry's sister, cooked and cared for Henry and their two younger brothers. She was extremely thin and tired-looking. She acted too adultlike for a seven-year-old.

Martha should have had someone caring for her and playing with her, but she was forced to be mother and nurse to her three young brothers. She couldn't even leave the house to be with other little girls at Bible club. No one else would stay home.

Day after day, for three months, Henry lay on a mattress, covered only with a dirty blanket. His baby brothers slept in the same room on another filthy blanket. They crawled naked over the grimy floors playing with their two dogs in the rat-infested apartment.

We brought Henry coloring books, toys and games. We were the only ones who played with him.

Henry is now back in Bible club. He loves his teachers' attention and affection. But each week after club he returns to that depressing tenement. No mother. No attention. No love. His legs are healed, but the scars inside may never heal.

ABANDONMENT

Abandonment is the most odious form of rejection. It is the ultimate insult between humans. That is why we were so grieved to find two sisters, ages three and six, roaming the caustic streets begging for food. We took them back to their ghetto apartment and discovered a scene of horror.

As the door was pushed open, the stench of decay was overpowering. Crumbling furniture, dirty clothes and garbage were everywhere. The broken refrigerator was cluttered with rotten food. Maggots wriggled and fell from shelf to shelf. There was no running water. The toilet and bathtub were full of human waste.

But the worst was yet to be discovered.

A soft whimpering cry came from behind a flimsy door. We hated to look—but we knew we had to. Inside the dark, unheated room lay a one-year-old baby girl, completely naked and surrounded by her own vomit and waste. This abandoned infant was so weak she could hardly cry.

Our stomachs turned. We could barely look. We wanted to turn and run, to pretend this was not real.

But we couldn't.

One of the police officers we called had grown up in that same neighborhood. He faced horrifying scenes almost every day. But when he saw this apartment and these children, he broke down and cried.

No one knows the long-term effects of such tragedies. But insecurity, self-depreciation and fear are likely results of being abandoned by one's parents.

Other parents, though equally remiss, abandon their children without leaving them.

Nineteen-year-old Susan was a heroin addict, drug pusher and prostitute. The day her son Hasaan was born, Susan was too high on drugs to care.

How unfair! When my wife, Katie, gave birth to our twins, Joshua and Paul, I almost burst with joy. A grin graced my face for days. I hugged and cuddled each of these precious gifts we had received from God. I didn't want to put them down. I never wanted this celebration of life to end.

By contrast, Hasaan spent the first days of his life being "detoxed," withdrawing from his prenatal addiction to narcotics. He appeared mildly retarded and showed signs of brain damage.

Hasaan's grandmother, uncles and four of his aunts plus their 10 children lived in a dilapidated, noisy tenement. His aunts knew from the beginning that Hasaan would be their responsibility. They invited us, their children's Bible club teachers, to a baby shower for him. Hasaan's mother walked through the room once with a 50-year-old junkie, Hasaan's father. She did not even acknowledge our presence. Worse yet, she ignored Hasaan.

For all intents and purposes Susan has abandoned Hasaan.

ABUSE

Gladys appeared to belong to a model family. She and her five brothers and sisters lived with their father and mother. Her father had a job. Her mother even invited us to conduct our Bible clubs in their home. But the facade of normality masked a reign of terror.

Gladys's father raped his four daughters regularly. He threatened to shoot them if they ever told anyone. They feared it would kill their sickly mother, who had high blood pressure, if she knew what their father was doing to them.

Gladys's father started raping her when she was nine. Almost every night for years he woke her and had sex with her on a sleeping bag on the kitchen floor. Her sedated mother never found out.

When Gladys was 13 she joined our Bible club in Watts, sang in our choir and seemed very interested in the Lord. She loved her Bible teacher but never shared about her father's continuing abuse. However, two years later Gladys dropped out of Bible club.

Shortly after that Gladys mysteriously gained 80 pounds. Severe stomach pain finally forced her to see a doctor. She feared that she might have a dead baby inside her. But the physician discovered huge tumors on her ovaries, the result of having had sex as a child. Gladys wept when she learned that both ovaries had died and she would never be able to have children.

After Gladys had recovered from her surgery, her father again demanded sex. Gladys was repulsed and could not stand it any longer. She felt like killing him.

Finally the night of horror came. Gladys's father approached her as he had done a hundred times before. But this time Gladys started to cry and became hysterical. She completely lost control, gasping for breath as she screamed at her warped father.

Gladys's father was infuriated. He grabbed his pistol

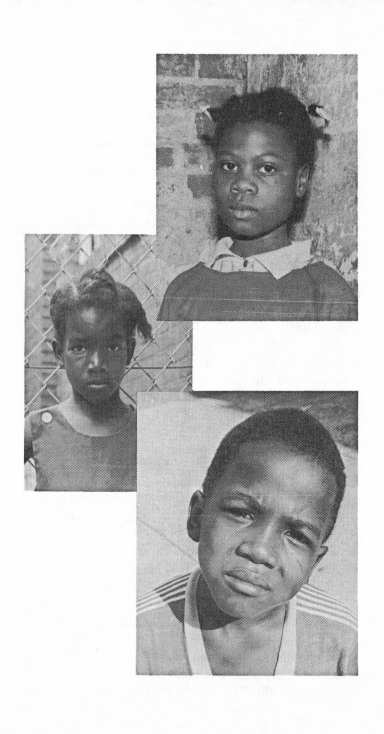

and yelled at his children to line up in a row. Then he pointed the loaded weapon at them as he lectured them about "respect." He threatened to shoot them one at a time if they did not apologize and obey him immediately.

Somehow Gladys's sister escaped, ran to a neighbor's house and called the police. The officers arrived just as the father was leaving. The children tearfully described their father's sexual abuse and the incidents that led to his threatening their lives. It was as if they were reliving those nights of terror.

Gladys's father denied everything. His kids were simply being disciplined. There had been no sexual abuse—no gun. He didn't even own a gun.

The children panicked. How could they prove what their father had done? What if they couldn't prove it? Then what would he do?

Somehow in the commotion Gladys's father had managed to hide his gun. If that weapon could only be found, the police might believe the children. They searched frantically for the pistol. Finally, the police discovered the weapon in the backyard and arrested their father.

While Gladys's father was in jail her mother died of a heart attack. Gladys was besieged with guilt. If only she had not refused her father, he would never have been arrested. Then her mother never would have found out about the perversion that broke her heart—and she would still be alive.

To add insult to tragedy, the children had no money to bury their mother. So they went from door to door in the housing project, one of the poorest neighborhoods in America, trying to collect donations to pay for their mother's funeral.

My heart broke when I found out about this obscenity. I phoned my friend Ted Engstrom at World Vision, who immediately sent the necessary money so that we could help pay for the funeral and end the repulsive spectacle of children begging for nickels and dimes to bury their mother.

After the funeral Gladys felt alone and worthless. She had no income and could not get a job. She had barely completed the tenth grade.

Gladys only knew one thing she could do—the only thing her father had taught her. She began prostituting.

FEAR

Everybody's afraid in the ghetto. Sometimes the fear stems from events or people outside of one's acquaintance—thieves, addicts or gang members. Other times, tragically, the fear results from one's own flesh and blood.

More than once, four-year-old Junior has nearly been beaten to death. He is permanently scarred and painfully thin. He does not know why he is so bad, or exactly what causes his mom to whip him. But he does know that once she gets started, she cannot stop.

Sylvia, Junior's mother, confesses, "I want to do right to my kids, but if somebody starts trouble with me, something snaps and I go crazy."

Junior has been hospitalized and placed in court custody to protect him from his alcoholic mother. But he always returns home. And every day he hears the same destructive accusations: "You're no good, boy. You ain't going nowhere. You're worthless."

Sylvia's "sometimes" husband Charles is a chronic and abusive alcoholic. Sylvia is the most frequent object of his violence. No matter where she hides Charles finds her. And Junior silently observes her humiliation, knowing exactly how his mother feels.

One time Charles beat Sylvia so badly that she lost the child she was carrying—his child—in her eighth month. Both grief and relief were in Sylvia's eyes as she related,

"I'm glad my child died. Even though I could feel her inside me I'm glad she didn't have to grow up in this mess. She's better off where she is now."

Sylvia continued, "A lot of times I think things would be better if I just shot myself and my children. If you knew the things I go through in a day, you wouldn't want to live either."

Sylvia's plight seemed irreparable. But we could not lose hope. We had to have enough faith for ourselves and for her.

So we loved and counseled Sylvia. We listened for hours as she poured out her heart. We cried with her, held her and loved her. Over and over again we shared that God was ready to meet her, to help her carry her burdens, to give her a fresh hope and a new start.

Finally Sylvia committed her life to Christ. She determined to live for God no matter how hard it might be. She began reading the Bible to her children and trying to respond to them in love.

But Charles did not change. He would come home drunk, snatch the Bible and throw it across the room.

After each beating Sylvia pleaded with God to help her and to change her situation. She tried to trust God, to wait for His intervention, but the beatings continued. Finally, in despair she cried, "God's not answering my prayers!"

That same night when Charles began his brutal routine Sylvia grabbed a butcher knife and stabbed him four times. He dropped to the floor. The knife had pierced within inches of his heart. Charles lived, but Sylvia decided she would never let him back into the house.

Charles, however, was determined to return. During one of his attempts to break into Sylvia's apartment, Junior listened to the vulgar screaming and trembled as Charles threatened to tear them to pieces. Sylvia called the police.

The officers would not come unless Charles had a gun. So Sylvia said he did. When the police arrived and found that Charles did not have a weapon, they took both Charles and Sylvia to jail.

We wanted to cry in frustration. It seemed so unfair that Sylvia had to lie to get the attention of the police and that she was punished for trying to protect herself.

Sylvia sleeps with a butcher knife by her bed and talks openly in front of Junior about killing Charles if he does get in. She rarely leaves the apartment. Junior is cautious when he plays outside. He's afraid that Charles will grab him for the house key that is tied around his neck.

Fear is contagious, self-perpetuating. Junior is afraid of Sylvia. Both Sylvia and Junior are afraid of Charles. No doubt Charles is afraid too.

Why?

Day after day, week after week I watch our Bible club children suffer from the uncontrolled anger of bitter, broken parents. I cry with the prophet, "Why do you make me look at injustice? Why do you tolerate wrong?" (Hab. 1:3).

Nine-year-old Renea was playing in the front yard with her father. It was one of those days that every child hopes for, a memory Renea would always cherish. Suddenly she saw her mother's car coming around the corner. As Renea turned and lifted her hand to wave, she saw her mother's new boyfriend in the car.

Renea's heart stopped. Every new man in her mother's life meant more trouble, more fear.

Before Renea could say anything she heard a shot. When she turned around, she saw that her daddy had fallen to the ground. Renea's mother drove off and left Renea's father lying in a pool of blood at the little girl's feet.

Renea's mother was arrested for first-degree murder. When Renea realized she had to testify in court she was terrified.

Renea did not know whether to tell the truth or to lie. She had loved her daddy, but she also loved her mommy. She never wanted to have to choose between them. And now she was about to lose them both.

Renea's father is dead. Her mother is in prison. Renea is afraid of the future.

Is It Hopeless?

Proverbs 22:6 says, "Train a child in the way he should go, and when he is old he will not turn from it." While this truth is a source of comfort and security for millions of godly parents, the inverse of this law has a chilling effect on the hurting children of the ghetto.

If youngsters experience neglect, rejection, abuse or fear in their formative years, aren't they likely to copy this model and become unfit parents themselves?

Childhood experiences radically affect who people become. In childhood, habits are estabished, role models are copied and character traits are formed. Children who are loved by their parents become secure, healthy adults. Abused youngsters become child abusers. Illegitimate children have youngsters out of wedlock. Beaten children become violent. Rejected young people reject others.

We reproduce after our own kind. As Galatians 6:7 says, "we reap what we sow." First and Second Kings repeatedly asserts, "He did evil in the eyes of the Lord, as his father had done." The model—good or bad—seems to be passed from generation to generation.

After three and four generations of immorality and broken homes, what hope is there?

Virtually none, unless there is divine intervention.

SECTION TWO
INCARNATIONAL LIVING

"And [Christ] was made flesh, and dwelt among us, (and we beheld his glory, the glory as of the only begotten of the Father,) full of grace and truth."

John 1:14, *KJV*

Every burning tenement in our inner cities means more homeless people, more broken families, more poverty and more shattered dreams burnt to ashes.

3
BECOMING ONE WITH THE COMMUNITY

The broken home did not appear in the inner city overnight. The spiritual, social and economic factors that led to its disintegration can be traced back to the infamous years of slavery in America. Character is not built in a day, neither is it destroyed in a day.

Consequently a long-term strategy is needed to transform families that have been shattered for decades into whole, healthy units. The mandatory foundation upon which this strategy must be built is incarnational living. Christians cannot minister in absentia.

This is why World Impact came to the inner city. It is why all of our missionaries who minister in the ghetto live in the ghetto. Living where we minister is an extension of the Incarnation. When God had an important message for man He clothed Himself with flesh and dwelt among us.

Then we beheld His glory! People in the inner city need to behold God.

A TEST OF FIRE

Tim and Janet Goddu live next door to our Newark Youth Center. At 3:00 A.M. blaring sirens interrupted their sound sleep. They ran outside to find a blazing fire. The three-story apartment one yard from their home was like a huge torch, completely engulfed in flames which leapt 30 feet above the roof.

Snow was falling. The windchill factor had dropped to 30 degrees below zero. Fifty people were standing on the icy street in their nightclothes.

Because Tim and Janet live where they minister no one had to inform them that there was an emergency. They knew. No one had to wait to ask for help. They were there. Tim and Janet were available to meet the needs of their crisis-ridden community 24 hours a day.

Tim immediately opened our Youth Center. Janet mixed hot chocolate. They emptied our supply of sweaters, socks, coats and gloves for their neighbors who had lost everything. It was incredibly sad that so many of our friends were suffering at once.

Suddenly the electricity, heat and phone in our Center went dead. The people panicked and rushed outside. They were sure that the Center was catching fire, too. But when they saw it was not, they came back in. We lit the Center with candles and flashlights.

We asked one lady if everyone had escaped unharmed. She answered, "Yes, except the old lady on the third floor. She didn't make it."

Seventy-two-year-old "Miss Ann" was like everybody in that building, a good friend and neighbor to us. We saw her nearly every day and were horrified that she had been trapped in that inferno.

The fire was out of control. We watched as the wall of the flaming structure crashed into Tim's house and then fell onto parked cars. Sparks repeatedly hit Tim's roof. The fireman kept hosing it down.

Five other major fires were blazing in Newark at the exact same time. For 20 minutes the water pressure was reduced to a dribble. Firemen frantically ran hoses from blocks away seeking more pressure as the fire raged on.

Inside the Center our neighbors were quiet. No one cried or said a word about losing absolutely everything they owned. This had happened to most of them before. They were thankful to get out alive.

But 14-year-old Denean stood dejectedly beside her mother. She did not know where her father was. Many people had seen him come out of the apartment, but no one knew where he had gone. It was strange that he was not with his family. Had he possible gone back into the burning building, looking for Denean?

A young mother came in with her one-year-old son wrapped in a blanket. She had been standing in the freezing street with no socks on. Her baby was just recovering from pneumonia. He was stone quiet, still weak from his sickness.

Janet went back home to find more socks. By now her house was also fire-damaged and flooded with water. It was beautiful to watch Janet bending down to put socks on this terrified mother who was staring bitterly ahead. Most people would have been worried about losing their own possessions, but Janet was caring for others.

The workmen found Miss Ann's body the next day. Denean's father still had not returned, so they worked for several days in the terrible cold and snow, sifting through debris looking for his body. They finally discovered what little there was left of it.

The fire was hard on the Goddus, yet God brought good out of the tragedy. A new closeness developed as

Tim and Janet supplied furniture, food, clothes and shelter for their neighbors.

Tim and Janet's house had been partially burned. Many of their possessions had been damaged or destroyed. But their peace, joy and love in the midst of personal crisis spoke more loudly to their neighbors of God's sufficiency than a thousand sermons.

Mrs. Anderson commented, "Now I know Christ can be real in this community. I've never seen it before. Now I believe."

Living in the neighborhood allowed Tim and Janet to model godly actions and responses even under adverse conditions. In terms of identifying with their neighbors Tim and Janet passed their test of fire with flying colors.

AN ANSWERED PRAYER

I am so glad the Goddus were there to help in Jesus' name. They were an answer to prayer!

Twenty years earlier I had wandered into an area of Los Angeles—not famous yet—called Watts and had started a Bible club for six boys in a federal housing project. Not one of those boys knew who his father was. I don't mean he didn't live with his father. I mean he had no idea who had fathered him. Each of those youngsters had at least one sister who was a prostitute, and one brother who was a pimp or a pusher.

But the most surprising thing to me was that not one of those children had ever sat down to a family meal. The family unit had so disintegrated that the tradition of breaking bread together had ceased.

The longer I ministered in Watts the more I began to understand the wretched consequences of the broken family in the inner city. I was overwhelmed. Despair and gloom tempted me to turn away, to write *Ichabod* ("no glory") over these apparently innocent victims.

Janet and Tim Goddu, World Impact missionaries in Newark, demonstrate incarnational living to their community and prove God's sufficiency in adversity when their own faith in Christ is tested by fire.

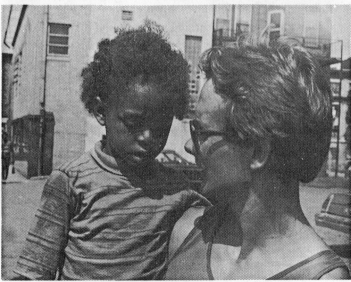

Tim Goddu and new friend from Newark Youth Center.

For generations God's resident lights on this planet had fled the ghetto, significantly dimming His witness. Ministering alone in the inner city was precarious. A solitary spark was very susceptible to being blown out.

Deep inside I knew that Jesus was the light of the whole world, not just the light of suburbia. My inner-city neighbors needed to experience this light. Then hope could be restored, sin could be forsaken and the abundant life could be realized.

I began to pray that God would send committed Christians—single adults, married couples, people from all walks of life—who would move into the ghetto and join me in illuminating the path to God.

Tim and Janet were part of God's answer.

While Tim was working as an accountant in New York City, Janet began looking for a job through which she could help people. She found World Impact listed under "religious organizations" in the phone book.

Janet had hoped to find an 8 A.M. to 5 P.M. job, so she was a bit taken back when she learned that our missionaries live right in the community where they serve in order to be available at all times.

But as Janet reflected on the implications of a commuter outreach the thought of becoming one with the community made sense. If Janet came and went at will, those to whom she ministered would never be sure that Janet could walk with God if she lived where they did.

Janet exclaimed, "Joining World Impact sounds like becoming a foreign missionary." And she was correct. While ministering in the inner city does not demand a trip across the ocean, it does require a journey into a different culture.

Tim was launching what promised to be an outstanding career in finance. He had studied and worked for so long that Janet was timid about even suggesting that Tim might give up his position in order to become a missionary. Ministering with us seemed highly improbable, yet the Spirit kept tugging at Janet's heart.

Janet asked if she and Tim could visit, so they could pray together more intelligently about how they could best become involved in bringing God's love to the inner city. And besides, she wanted to expose Tim to our work.

Tim recalls, "I wanted to minister to the poor, but World Impact was asking for a huge commitment. I was very attracted to the staff members' love for the Lord and for each other and to the commitment to touching the oppressed. I was impressed by the Bible clubs, Bible studies and the tangible expressions of Christian love I saw at World Impact. But I was not ready to jump on board. At least, not yet."

Tim asked, "Would it be possible for Janet and me to make a commitment to minister *one afternoon* each week to the same children? We'll be here *every* week and we will be faithful to those youngsters."

Tim and Janet understood the importance of ongoing relationships and felt God calling them to minister with us. Since their lives reflected Christ's compassion and concern, we agreed.

Our staff immediately fell in love with the Goddus. And the Bible club children knew that Tim and Janet were God's special gift of love to them. Those inner-city youngsters hugged and kissed Tim and Janet with all the energy they could muster. Before long Tim and Janet were with us so often that they were almost like full-time staff.

After several months of active involvement with us God spoke clearly to the Goddus. Tim resigned from his accounting job and they moved into the inner city to minister with us.

The Goddus now live on Eighth Street in Newark. They have seen the distinction between "us" and "you" fade away. When their neighbors were terrorized by a street gang, the Goddus were not exempt. Like the rest of the community Tim and Janet have been burglarized. And when their neighbors' house caught on fire, so did theirs.

Tim and Janet have become one with the community.

BECOMING FRIENDS

Once people in the neighborhood accepted Tim and Janet deep friendships developed. Jay was one of Tim's Bible club students. Jay lived with his 44-year-old mother, Roberta, in a two-story, wood-framed house that should have been condemned. It had broken windows, rotting floors, crumbling ceilings and faulty wiring.

Roberta was an alcoholic who had arthritis and liver problems. The phlebitis in her right leg forced her to walk with a brace.

When Jay took me to meet his mother, her breath smelled of alcohol. Her face and body had aged beyond her years. Two of her oldest boys were in trouble with the law. As Roberta talked it became obvious that Jay was her sole reason for living. He was her pride and joy.

We stood in the kitchen, which a gas stove heated to barely 30 degrees. There was no water in the home. The pipes had frozen solid and broken, flooding the basement. The main shut-off valve at the street level was frozen.

In the evenings Jay slept at Tim's house. Roberta stayed with neighbors, drinking to ease the pain, until about midnight. Then she slept in a sleeping bag covered with seven blankets in her kitchen.

Tim and Janet's relationship with Roberta and Jay deepened. Roberta loved to cook meals for the Goddus. Twice a month Roberta rode along and did her food shopping with Janet. Roberta often used Janet's washing machine.

Jay remained committed in his love for the Lord in spite of the decrepit housing, the freezing winters, the shortage of food, the dirty clothes and the mother who loved him but could not lick the bottle. Jay's gentle, sweet, steadfast spirit reminded me of Tim.

Then Roberta developed cancer. For a year and a half she was in and out of the hospital, often staying in six to eight weeks at a time. Tim and Janet graciously opened their home to Jay. He became like a son.

While in the hospital Roberta became a Christian. For six months Tim and Janet visited Roberta almost every afternoon before Bible clubs to read the Bible, pray and just be with her. Often they came home elated at her good spirit and humor; often they returned discouraged by her gradual weakening and inevitable death.

Roberta asked the Goddus to be Jay's guardians. When Roberta died Tim and Janet took complete responsibility for Jay. Sometimes availability turns into a full-time job.

Jay worked his way through high school and was very involved in our ministry. Then he enrolled at a state college. Because Tim and Janet were available, Roberta is spending eternity in heaven and Jay has a bright future.

Janet Goddu serves the children of Newark in love.

In Los Angeles, rural Canadian Fred Stoesz and his family serve as urban missionaries to inner-city families. They model stability, faithfulness and love to those knowing only fractured relationships.

4
A REAL LIFE EXAMPLE

Another special person God sent to represent Him was Fred Stoesz. On the surface Fred looked like an unlikely candidate. He had grown up in rural Canada and had spent more time during his years at Bible School skiing, playing hockey and riding motorcycles than he had spent studying theology.

But Fred had been reared in a godly home and he could not ignore the truths of Scripture that he had heard for years. He came to Los Angeles in 1974 intending to stay for one year. But the work never seemed to be completed, the relationships never at a point at which he could afford to leave. Many lonely children, teenagers and adults saw Fred as their first real friend. They needed someone who would remain committed to them.

Now, over a decade later, Fred is still here and he has no intention of leaving.

A CHRISTIAN "FATHER"

If ever there was a light that reflected God's love it was Fred. His practical faith in the Lord, his happy, optimistic spirit and his deep security in God's ultimate control readily attracted people to the Father.

Fred met his wife Jolene in Los Angeles. She was also a World Impact missionary. They are now raising a family, right here in the inner city. For a community in which a husband and wife living together and raising all their children together is a rarity, Fred is worth observing. His life and demeanor inspire hope in all who are around him.

One object of World Impact's ministry is to build healthy family units in the inner city. But children who have never met their father or have never seen parents function as a loving, committed team have a difficult time becoming godly spouses and parents. They cannot reproduce what they have never seen. People learn better by observing than merely by listening.

The greatest advantage to living where we minister is modeling. We know who God wants us to be because Jesus provided us with a living illustration. Now through us, Jesus is showing others who God wants them to be.

A CHRISTIAN "SON"

Terrel is a splendid example of an inner-city teen who is patterning his life after a godly man.

One Sunday evening sticks out in my memory. We had taken our Los Angeles teen choir to Skyline Wesleyan Church in San Diego. Terrel stood up to testify to his faith in Christ. He shared about being one of 13 children. His father, who was not living at home, had been shot and killed. Two years later his mother died in a tragic car accident.

Terrel moved from Texas to Los Angeles to live with his sister, her husband and seven children in a small home. Terrel began attending our weekly Bible club and soon accepted Christ.

As Terrel matured he joined a covenant group with several other committed Christian teenagers. They met regularly to study, pray and share their needs and victories. They covenanted to stand with each other through thick and thin and to remind one another of God's principles. They promised to share their burdens and to uphold each other in prayer.

Terrel related to the congregation, "Bible club and this choir bring me great joy and take the place of the real family which I never had."

Then Terrel said, "But the person I really love is Fred."

Terrel's voice began to crack, "He's like a father to me. I just love spending time with Fred and Jolene and their little boy, Aaron. When I grow up I want to be just like . . . . "

Terrel never finished. He broke down and cried like a baby.

I sat in that congregation and along with most of the other people wept with Terrel. He never finished saying everything he wanted to, but he communicated in a way that words could not.

Terrel saw Christ in Fred. Terrel loved the way Fred loved his family, the way Fred related to his neighbors and the manner in which Fred lived God's love. And Terrel wanted to be like Fred.

Terrel's respect for Fred had not been acquired overnight. Fred was Terrel's Bible club teacher. They sang together in choir. They worked together, played together, prayed together and eventually lived together.

For a year and a half, Terrel spent virtually every weekend at Fred's home. Fred taught Terrel that being part of a family included having responsibilities. Terrel washed dishes, helped maintain the yard and even learned to baby-sit.

One summer Fred took Terrel and some of our other Christian teenagers on a wilderness expedition. Fred was praying that their extended time together would significantly deepen their faith in God and commitment to each other.

None of Fred's teenagers will forget the mountain climbing. The guys were amazed that Fred expected them to scale that "huge mountain." Slowly they made their way higher and higher at an angle that appeared to them to be straight up. The braver guys laughed at the more cautious. But everybody made it to the top.

However, their initial sighs of relief and feelings of accomplishment were short-lived once they saw what was on the other side. Our inner-city teens gasped when they realized that Fred expected them to rappel down that sheer cliff.

One guy yelled, "I ain't never goin' nowhere with you again!"

Another cried, "You're trying to kill me, man! There ain't no way I'm gonna do that."

When Fred assured them that they would be fastened to ropes Terrel immediately pointed out that ropes had been known to break and it was a 100-foot drop. Fred gave a brilliant speech on bravery, maybe as much for his own benefit as for the teens.

Finally Terrel gingerly stepped backwards over the edge and rappeled to the bottom perfectly. Fred was relieved that Terrel hadn't turned upside down. Some of the later guys did.

Every night Fred brought into focus the biblical applications of the lessons that were learned during the day.

The long grueling hikes in Yosemite underscored the endurance that was essential for a believer's consistent walk with God. Rappeling down a steep mountain illustrated the absolute faith a Christian needed to place in God. During those times Terrel learned, "The Christian life takes all you've got."

One afternoon while the guys were hiking they got caught in a tremendous hailstorm. Since they had tied large tarps over their camping area they eagerly looked forward to diving into their dry sleeping bags when they returned. Everyone was freezing by the time they finally reached their campsite. But to their dismay the tents had collapsed under three inches of hail.

Slowly they dug out what was left of their camp. They mournfully looked at Fred. He just smiled. Finally they made a momentous decision. Two fully-grown teenagers squeezed into each sleeping bag because they thought they would freeze to death if they didn't. Fred nearly died laughing. Those tough street dudes were timid mountain men. By the end of the trip God had answered Fred's prayers. There was a stronger commitment to God and a fresh unity among all the guys.

Later that summer Fred encouraged Terrel to get a part-time job. Terrel learned how to save money and experienced the joy of giving to others. Before long he was also helping us teach four-, five- and six-year-olds in one of our Bible clubs. Terrel related, "I'm really proud when those little kids run up and say, 'Hi, Bible teacher!'"

In so many ways Terrel is becoming like Fred. Terrel has the same exuberance for life, the same trusting spirit, the same love for God.

If imitation is the greatest form of flattery, Terrel has paid Fred the ultimate compliment.

5
WE'LL ALWAYS BE HERE

Susie Krehbiel has always been a go-getter. She served as student body president at Wichita State University and intended to go to law school in order to become a judge. She wanted God to use her to help ensure justice for the oppressed.

Susie loved God with all her heart and sincerely wanted to do whatever would bring Him the most honor and glory. During her senior year of college God began speaking to Susie about a more personal involvement with the poor and oppressed. After visiting our Wichita ministry she knew that God wanted her to live and teach the gospel in America's inner cities.

At first Susie thought she would give one or two years of her life to inner-city missions and then pursue her legal career. But we explained that our missionaries continue

ministering with us at least until they have trained someone from the inner city to take over the ministry they
began. This is the bottom line of discipleship—equipping
others to teach others (see 2 Timothy 2:2).

We explained to Susie that quite honestly, training
indigenous leadership could take 10 years, 20 years or
even a lifetime. We knew that in this unstable culture nothing impedes a young believer's journey to maturity more
than a frequent change of missionaries.

We had learned that the hard way.

HIT-AND-MISS RELATIONSHIPS

After ministering alone for a couple of years in Watts, I
recruited hundreds of college volunteers to conduct
weekly Bible clubs for inner-city children. The youngsters
idolized the collegians. When a Bible club teacher would
say, "I love you and God loves you. I'm going to teach you
about Jesus every week," the children accepted those
words as gospel.

But after a year, most of the college students would
graduate or be transferred to a different Christian service
assignment. So when the children were just beginning to
trust and depend on their new-found friends, the college
students would disappear. The children felt betrayed.

For most of the youngsters these Bible teachers had
been the first "picture" of God they had ever seen. And
when the college students failed to return, the children felt
that God Himself had deserted them.

I tried to explain that these college students had other
important things to do; the youngsters had not caused
their teachers to leave. But the children always felt
rejected and sometimes guilty. Some of them were sure
that if they had not acted up during the Bible lessons their
teachers would never have left.

Many of these youngsters had been abandoned by

their fathers, neglected by their mothers or passed from one relative to another. They believed that somehow *they* must have caused all that rejection.

Years of trying to explain the impossible to hundreds of heartbroken children confirmed our fear that shallow hit-and-miss relationships often did more harm than good. Once a trust is betrayed, children are much less likely to open up to another "here today, gone tomorrow" Bible teacher.

These children deserved better. They needed stable, lasting friendships with godly men and women after whom they could model their lives. Only an ongoing ministry could counteract the instability of the ghetto.

ACCEPTING A CHALLENGE

After much prayer and godly counsel, Susie began to understand the necessity of long-term relationships. She realized that the hurting people in the ghetto would not be helped significantly by one or two years of ministry. Our Bible club students came from broken homes. They needed stable, loving teachers who would stand with them through childhood, adolescence and adulthood in order to be nurtured to maturity. This strong support system and stabilizing influence would produce godly parents and complete families.

Susie recalls, "I understood that becoming an inner-city missionary would demand all the energy, creativity and commitment that God could produce through me. It would be a great challenge. But I liked that. And I knew this was one place where God could stretch my faith and increase my dependence upon Him."

A year after graduation Susie decided to join our staff. She moved into the inner city of Los Angeles as a missionary and began to minister to Sue Mitchell, a young woman who had grown up in the housing projects of Los Angeles.

Sue Mitchell had accepted Christ in one of our early Bible clubs while we were still using college volunteers as teachers. How Sue loved her teacher! Sue memorized Bible verses, sang Christian songs and did everything she could to please God—and her teacher. The highlight of Sue's week was when that big yellow bus, jammed with Christian college students, pulled into the projects. That signaled the beginning of a special time of love and personal attention.

Then one Saturday morning the Bible teachers did not show up for club. As a matter of fact they never returned. Sue was heartbroken. She no longer had a special friend with whom to share her fears and hurts. There were no more Bible stories, no singing, no crafts. Sue thought, "Maybe they didn't really love me. Maybe I was just a 'project.'"

Sue returned to Bible club only after we made a commitment to having long-term missionaries. We promised Sue, "We'll always be here." She recommitted her life to Christ and has continued to grow in the Lord for the past 12 years.

When Sue Mitchell's love for God became evident we invited her to join our staff. Susie Krehbiel began training Sue to minister. They lived together, taught together and prayed together. They struggled through the hard times and rejoiced in the goodness of God.

Both women knew the importance of permanence. Sue reminded us, "It's just not fair to lead a youngster to Christ and then leave her all alone in her new Christian life. You can't call it love when you say, 'God bless you. I hope everything works out okay,' and then leave. We have to reflect the faithfulness of our Father."

Susie added, "Sometimes young people who have been solidly grounded in God's Word will stray from His will. But because of our continued presence in the community they know that when they turn again to God, we will be here to affirm them and to help them."

At Christmastime, 1984, Sue and Susie moved back into Watts. They live three doors away from the federal housing project where Sue had first heard about Jesus 18 years earlier. Sue knows the potential dangers, hurts and frustrations of living in such a deprived neighborhood. But she said, "This Christmas the gift I want to give to others is myself. I give myself to be the hands and feet of Jesus in Watts."

By purchasing a home and moving into Watts our actions clearly announced to the boys and girls, the teenagers and adults that we will always be here. God has been completely faithful to the work He began years ago in Sue's life through a Bible club. We will be here for the hundreds who will follow in Sue's footsteps.

Two dedicated World Impact staffers, Sue Mitchell (left) and Susie Krehbiel, witness Christ through a Bible club outreach to their Watts neighborhood.

Moving from rural Kansas to Wichita's inner city, Al Ewert's gentle manner and friendly spirit have led him into a life-changing outreach to teenagers.

6
WHATEVER IT TAKES

One of the first things our missionaries have to learn is flexibility. Not everything works out the way they think it should. Not everything is the way it appears.

Al Ewert was like most of the people God brought to minister in the inner city. He came from a "normal" background. He grew up like you and me. His father was a college registrar; his mother, a church secretary.

THE SHIRT OFF YOUR BACK

When Al moved from rural Kansas into the inner city of Wichita the teenagers in his community were immediately attracted to his warm, friendly spirit. And in the early years they often took advantage of his gentleness. Teenagers appeared eager to study the Bible at Al's house. But after their Bible studies, Al would often find his dresser drawers empty.

The Tabor College T-shirts hanging on Al's neighbor's clotheslines looked out of place. Al's alma mater was not exactly a well-known school in the inner city. But Al never had the nerve to retrieve his shirts.

One of Al's T-shirts had been stolen by Jimmy, a guy who had never been accused of having an abundance of common sense. As if to prove the point, Jimmy had the audacity to complain to Al, "Some bum swiped my Tabor T-shirt."

Al recalls, "I often had to change the subject when my mother would ask me how I liked the new shirt she had given me for Christmas. New clothes seldom lasted more than two weeks. Once somebody even stole all my underwear."

Walt was one of the men who ministered with Al. One day a guy we hardly knew walked into Al's home. All of a sudden Walt exclaimed: "You've got my pants on!"

Walt had had enough. Most of his clothes had been stolen by street guys who were constantly hanging out at Al's place. All Walt had left was torn jeans. Walt was mad enough and big enough that the guy did exactly what Walt told him. Walt made our visitor take off his pants right on the spot. I don't remember how the guy got home.

If losing a shirt, a pair of pants, a car battery or a camera would have driven Al away, he would have lost before he had begun. The value of the broken lives around Al was far greater than a few material possessions. Al soon learned that if he was going to be successful in raising up urban disciples, he would not only have to go the extra mile, he would have to do *whatever it takes*.

WHAT A DEAL

When I first came to the city I was forever getting flat

tires. But the strangest thing always occurred. Some guy would wander by right when I was looking at the flat and say that he just happened to have an extra tire back home that would fit my car—and he'd give me a break and let me have it for $5. Of course I could never touch a tire for $5 anywhere else.

But soon I understood that I had been marked as a pigeon. Those guys had been sticking a penknife into my tires and then selling me replacements they had stolen off someone else's car.

In the city, people can deliver virtually anything you want for any price you can afford to pay. They can, that is, if you don't mind buying stolen merchandise.

I remember the day that Al bought this long leather coat for $10. Al was proud as punch about the deal he had gotten. But he could not figure out why all the guys in the neighborhood chuckled when he told them about it—until someone finally explained to Al that his coat was "hot."

Periodically new missionaries would show up with watches, stereos, tires and everything imaginable that they had purchased for an unbelievable price. Our patronizing their questionable "business ventures" one day and sharing Christ with them the next left several street vendors profoundly confused.

WHAT A COVER

Al had met Nickey before Nickey became a heroin addict. When he entered a methadone program to break his addiction he needed a place to stay. Al thought Nickey was close to accepting Christ so Al invited him to move in.

Al got a little suspicious when Nickey would disappear around the corner for 15 minutes and then return relaxed and smiling. But the clinic where he checked in every day had assured Al that they would phone if any trace of heroin showed up in Nickey's urine sample. They never called.

One day Al's street exploded with sirens. When Al ran to his front door he was astonished to see one squad car after another pull up. The entire block was filled with detectives and camera crews.

The police ran across the street from Al's house and pulled Al's neighbors out of their home. Officers with shot guns searched their car. Al could not believe what he was seeing. He knew that family. They were peaceful, law-abiding citizens.

Years later Al heard the rest of the story. The police had gone to the wrong address. They were supposed to have busted Al's house, where Nickey had been selling heroin. We had naively provided the ideal cover at our "Christian" home.

Nickey had been using heroin the whole time he had lived with Al. Nickey would get other guys to fill a bottle with urine which he would then sneak into the clinic. Nickey only lived with Al for a month, but that could have destroyed our ministry. Al still shudders at the thought of the police breaking down his door and questioning him on camera.

IMPROVING PUBLIC RELATIONS

A flood of street guys was always at Al's house that first year. They had been kicked out of school, or had been in jail or juvenile hall. Al thought it would be good for them to form a basketball team and play in a league. They needed this challenge. And they had a pretty good team when they played together and didn't revert to "street ball."

It was quite a sight to see Al drive his team to a game. These seven big dudes loved to "stare down" intimidated motorists who were next to them at stop lights. Embarrassed, Al stared straight ahead and prayed that nobody would recognize him.

Al's team won a few and lost a few. But they hated to lose. They were always convinced that they were better than the other team.

Al had to miss two games. Once he was sick and another time he had to speak at a church. Al mistakenly let his guys go to those games by themselves. The police were called to both contests. At the first one, Al's guys chased the referee down the street. The other time they cornered some opposing team members in the locker room.

That was the last year that we played in the Wichita Church League. To this day there may be certain churches which do not support our ministry because of that first basketball team.

HORSING AROUND

In spite of Al's experiences his love for these guys grew. He prayed for them by name. He taught them the Bible, fed them dinner, memorized Scripture with them and did everything he could to direct them to God. And many of these young men accepted Christ.

One year Al decided to take a group of young Christians to the Colorado Rockies for a trail ride. That would be a place where he could spend some quality time with his guys.

Few of these inner-city teenagers had ever ridden a horse. Nervously they talked to their horses, trying to make friends. They rode from three to five hours each day, ending up at a 10,000-foot elevation.

The nights were so cold that their water froze. The first evening the guys huddled in the tent, afraid of the darkness and the unfamiliar sounds of the animals. Mornings began early. They fed, watered and brushed down their animals. Periodically a guy would holler as a horse stepped on his foot.

Each night the guys sat around a large bonfire talking about the lessons they had learned, sharing Scripture, singing and praying together. As the initial fear wore off, they started sleeping out under the stars.

One night the teens were awakened by the noise of horses kicking each other. Suddenly the animals broke the ropes with which they were tied and got loose. Simultaneously a rainstorm hit. Terror struck our teens. The fear of losing their horses miles from the closest sign of civilization propelled them to action. There was no time to get dressed.

Thirteen inner-city teens in the middle of the night in freezing temperatures ran around in their underwear and boots yelling at each other, trying to find the horses. Al laughed so hard he got a stomachache.

Today Al cannot drive down a street in his community without people waving to him. They know that Al loves them with all his heart. If there is trouble or an emergency, they can go to Al. Somehow he will help. They have watched him be ripped off and used just as they have been. But after 14 years, Al is still there. That is enough for them. They know that Al will do whatever it takes.

GOD'S PEOPLE DOING GOD'S WORK

For the past two decades God has been sending His choice servants from all over the United States and Canada to America's inner cities. One even came from Viet Nam! They are godly men and women earnestly concerned about the plight of the poor and oppressed. They understand that there is no quick fix and they are willing to invest the rest of their lives here if needed. They have come from a rich variety of backgrounds: rural Canada, New York business offices, suburban colleges. Some were well-to-do, others were poor. Many were middle class. But they all share the same commitment to bring hope, love and salvation to America's ghettos. Their incarnational living is the foundation upon which their preaching, teaching and tangible Christian love stand.

Children gravitate naturally to Al Ewert. Here he and two young friends enjoy a warm moment together.

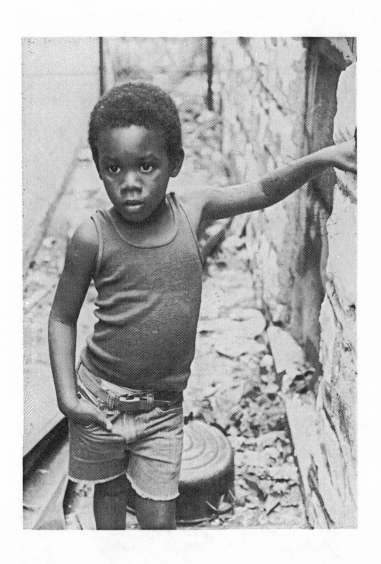

SECTION THREE
LIVING THE GOSPEL

"What good is it, my brothers, if a man claims to have faith but has no deeds? Can such faith save him? Suppose a brother or sister is without clothes and daily food. If one of you says to him, 'Go, I wish you well; keep warm and well fed,' but does nothing about his physical needs, what good is it? In the same way, faith by itself, if it is not accompanied by action, is dead."

James 2:14-17

Al Warren always manages to find time for the one who lacks companionship or needs a listening ear.

7

GIVING WITH NO STRINGS ATTACHED

Christ's declared purpose for His Incarnation was to preach the gospel to the poor, to heal the brokenhearted, to deliver the captives and to free the oppressed.

World Impact walks in the footsteps of the Nazarene in preaching and living out the implications of the gospel. This is especially urgent in a society riddled by broken families, encumbered by inadequate educational institutions, plagued by chronic unemployment and shamed by substandard housing.

FEELING GOOD, DOING GOOD

Ministry in the inner city is not all blood, sweat and tears. God showers our missionaries with great blessings and generous doses of encouragement amidst the heartbreaks.

A long-distance runner experiences exhilaration after completing an excruciating race. A mother feels joyful following a painful childbirth. Similarly a Christian feels good when his efforts bring hope to a hopeless situation.

The first time I took a Thanksgiving dinner—turkey, potatoes, vegetables and all the trimmings—to a poverty-stricken family was one of those memorable moments. The mother wept as she explained that without my caring they would have had nothing to eat. She truly believed that God had sent me and that He had met her need.

I was so touched by her genuine thankfulness I almost started to cry. I was supposed to be giving to her—but she gave far more to me. I will never forget the warm, full, abundant feeling. That rush of joy has been repeated hundreds of times. It never gets old.

Our missionaries share that same exhilaration every time they offer a cup of cold water in the name of the Master. It is a peace, joy and exuberance that money cannot buy. While this experience is not the reason for our giving, it is certainly a legitimate offspring of obeying God. Our tangible giving not only alleviates pain and suffering, it also brings us joy.

Food and Clothing

Our Bible club children frequently find themselves plagued by atrocious circumstances beyond their control. When those emergencies arise we respond immediately in the name of Jesus.

Starvation is not prevalent in the United States, but it is more common than most of us want to believe. Not long ago we met a four-year-old boy who was starving.

We found Rashaad sitting on our front porch. His movements were slow and sad, like those of an aging man. His tiny body made you look twice. Lots of children in the ghetto are skinny, but Rashaad was *too* skinny. He had gone without food so long that he did not even want to eat.

Rashaad's clothes were no more than dirty rags. He had no underwear or socks. On his right foot he wore a small, canvas shoe with holes in it. His left foot was swallowed up by a right-footed leather shoe that was at least three sizes too big. Neither shoe had laces.

We will never forget the hollow look in Rashaad's eyes. There was not even a spark of the usual mischief so common in four-year-olds. He did not smile. He did not want to play. When he tried to talk he barely whispered. All he wanted to do was sit on a Bible club teacher's lap and hold his hand. Rashaad was satisfied to just be close. And we had never seen him before.

Rashaad did not respond much to the new clothes and shoes that we gave him. But when we got him to eat a little he began to change. By the time he finished a peanut butter and jelly sandwich and some orange slices his eyes had brightened up. He began to talk. He even smiled.

When we walked Rashaad home to his fourth-floor apartment a party was going on. No one cared where he had been. He was the youngest of 11 children who lived with their invalid grandmother and mother. Their father had left six years earlier.

The family had three single beds for 13 people. They had one chest of drawers, but no refrigerator—no way of keeping food. When the mother was gone the older children would eat what food there was. The younger ones went hungry.

The same God who sent manna from heaven and multiplied the loaves and fishes provided food for Rashaad and his family that afternoon.

Temporary Housing

Al Warren experienced great joy when he shared his home with 10-year-old Demond, one of Al's most loving Bible club children.

Demond understands the degradation of poverty first-hand. His winter coat was so ragged that he had to attach the sleeves with pins. Other children saw the pins and continually pulled off the sleeves, forcing Demond to make the humiliating choice of playing tough and letting the sleeves go, or chasing the kids to retrieve the rest of his coat.

One Sunday evening after I had preached at a church service, I visited Demond. The front door was boarded up, so I had to crawl through a broken window in his condemned house to get in. I stumbled over the garbage and dilapidated furniture in the dark rooms, running my hand along the crumbling walls as a guide.

Water covered most of the floor. The water line had broken near the kitchen. Demond's two younger brothers were turning the water on and off from the main line in the basement. His older brother was upstairs filling pans with water for drinking and cooking.

Half of the windows were broken. A thin sheet of plastic from the dry cleaners was the only protection from the freezing weather outside. None of the boys had shoes on. Their mother was not home. She seldom was. Suddenly I understood why Al, Demond's Bible teacher, felt compelled to check on him every night.

Al told me about visiting Demond's home one evening at 9:00 P.M. He had brought blankets, food, shoes and warm clothing for each boy. Their mother was not home. Demond and his brothers were huddled near the small stove. The gas burners, which were going full blast, provided the only heat in the apartment.

It was so cold that Al could see his breath, even though he stood right next to the gas flames. Demond was shivering. All three boys were listless, staring off into space.

Al waited until after 10:00 P.M. Demond looked longingly at Al, wanting to go home with him. But Demond was afraid he would be beaten if he left without his mother's consent. No one knew when—or if—she would come home.

The youngsters spent that night waiting for her. She didn't return.

When the temperature fell below zero, we were compelled to do more. Demond's mother finally gave us permission to have the four youngest boys spend the cold nights in our homes.

We will never forget the first night. The boys were so excited you would have thought they were going to a circus. Demond obviously had never taken a shower before. He asked to take a second shower that same night! The children's clothes were layered with dirt and stank from repeated wearings. We had to wash them several times. The boys were delighted to go to bed early so that they could snuggle under clean, warm sheets and covers.

Providing temporary shelter for Demond was only a stopgap response. He desperately needs a permanent solution. He needs a warm bed, a new apartment before the old one burns down and a committed adult who will care for him and stay with him when he is frightened by the strange noises and eerie shadows at night.

Medical Attention

Scott McConaughey was greatly blessed when he was able to arrange for a badly needed operation for six-year-old Kim. Kim has a beautiful smile and soft, dark skin. Her short black hair is pulled back tight and held in place with a rubber band.

Kim, her brother and 22-year-old mother share a tenement with 26 people—five cousins, four uncles, six aunts and their boyfriends and girlfriends. Kim's life is crammed with violence, hatred and rejection.

Terrible memories haunt Kim.

Kim can't forget her uncle's screams after he placed what he mistakenly thought was an unloaded pistol against the head of his son, and squeezed the trigger.

Kim recalls the horror of her aunt's former boyfriend stabbing her present boyfriend with a steak knife.

Kim still hears the wailing of her 21-year-old neighbor who was robbed and then strangled to death right in Kim's building.

Kim is still wounded from the frequent beatings with hangers, belts and extension cords.

But most devastating, Kim can't forget being rejected by her parents. She sees her father, an addict and dealer, maybe once a year. Kim's mother, Monica, leaves for weeks at a time. Kim never knows where Monica is nor when she will return.

Monica completely forgot Kim's birthday, even though Monica had promised Kim a cake and a new doll. Kim did not attend kindergarten last year because Monica forgot to enroll her.

As if Monica's negligence was not enough Kim was being teased by her family and friends because she was cross-eyed. Our hearts broke for this precious child. So we arranged for a doctor to correct her condition.

When Kim was in the hospital Monica told her, "Kim, I have to leave for a minute, but I'll be right back to spend the night with you." Monica didn't return.

After Kim's operation, we even purchased the expensive patches that were necessary to facilitate the restoration of her eyesight. But Monica never remembered to put the patch over Kim's strong eye. Kim's sight is greatly improved, but it's not what it should be.

The long process of replacing the vicious nightmares with happy memories has begun. Because we cared enough to help correct Kim's vision she knows God loves her and we love her. Kim recently told her Bible teacher, "I love you. And I love Jesus, too!" A smile that was once crushed by circumstances beyond Kim's control finally had a reason to surface.

THE HANDS OF CHRIST

It is an honor and a blessing to be the hands of Christ in a hurting world. There are few places in the United States where the gospel can be so practically lived out. Every time an ounce of love is given, God returns it a hundred-fold.

We are committed to quickly responding to our neighbors' needs. Food, shoes, clothing, furniture, household utensils, heating oil, blankets, sleeping bags, shelter and medicine are our most common gifts. But we also help with plumbing, wiring, insulation, legal counsel and medical and dental work.

Poverty and oppression remain, but a beachhead of love and justice has been established. As God's people respond to His call to feed the hungry, shelter the destitute and heal the sick a full-scale invasion will be launched.

What a joy it is to responsibly demonstrate Christ's love in a hurting world. We remember the words of Jesus, "Whatever you did for one of the least of these brothers of mine, you did for me" (Matt. 25:40).

When the needs of hurting people are met without their begging, God is glorified. Winter-weight clothes, given to these children in Christ's name, protect both their health and their self-respect while assuring them that God and His Church care.

8

RESPONSIBLE GIVING

Galatians 6:10 (KJV) summarizes the cornerstone upon which Christian giving is founded: "Do *good* unto all men, especially unto them who are of the household of faith."

When I first came to the ghetto I received a rude awakening: Not all giving is "doing good." I gave some money to a hungry alcoholic who drank up my charity. I naively fed the habit of a teenage addict instead of her starving child. Even though I had good intentions I was not "doing good." Christian compassion includes the responsibility to ensure that your gifts build up, not destroy, the recipient.

For example, when my son David was an infant I compassionately carried him around because he was unable to walk. But if I had continued to carry David everywhere year after year for fear he might fall, stub his toe or wear himself out, the results would have been destructive.

David never would have learned to walk. His legs would have remained weak and uncoordinated. When he entered school he would have been completely dependent upon me to carry him. However pure my motivation, this nonrestrictive giving would have destroyed David.

MATURITY AND DIGNITY

We face similar situations when helping needy people in the city. A gift of food, clothing or medicine can be an act of compassion. But irresponsible giving can promote an unhealthy dependence which destroys the dignity of the recipients. And God is grieved, not glorified, when the recipients are "crippled" by our "kindness."

We have found that the following guidelines help to ensure responsible giving on our part.

1. Develop a Relationship with the Recipients

Our relationship with the Giver of "every good gift" (Jas. 1:17, *KJV*) provides a model for our relationship with our neighbors in need. Because God knows us perfectly, He can discern our true needs and meet them without hindering our growth.

When we know people well, we are aware when there is a need and can discern whether or not our gift will assist our friends to "become mature, attaining to the whole measure of the fullness of Christ" (Eph. 4:13).

God is glorified when the needs of hurting people are met without their begging for help. When we see children without coats in winter, teenagers unable to keep up with their school work or families without food, and answer those emergencies in Christ's name, our friends sense divine intervention.

We frequently explain, "God moved Christians to provide this food. Please accept it as a token of God's special love for you." The recipients are usually very interested in knowing about this God who is concerned about their practical needs. Handouts apart from relationships seldom lead people to God.

2. Build the Dignity of the Recipients

We guard the self-image of the recipients and protect our relationship with them by helping them maintain their self-respect. Two principles assist us in doing this:

a. The recipients contribute

When people receive something for nothing they value it accordingly. The boys who came to my first Bible club were excited as could be when I gave them their very own Bibles. I was thrilled with their immediate response. But when club was over Bibles littered the field where we had studied. The children had run off to play or had gone home, leaving their Bibles in the dirt, under a tree and on the benches.

I was hurt. Even though it had cost me only a few dollars to purchase these Bibles, money was tight. I felt betrayed, even a little angry. But God used this experience to teach me a valuable lesson.

The next week I asked the boys to bring their Bibles to club because they would need them to complete the lesson we would do together. I knew most of them did not have their Bibles. I did. I had collected them and had taken them home with me.

When the boys confessed that they had forgotten their Bibles, I told them that they could buy a Bible for one dollar. The following week every child but one brought his money. The boy who could not afford a dollar cleaned up the playground for me and "earned" his Bible.

Never again did I see those Bibles lying around. Now they were valuable, prized possessions.

Our club children pay a few dollars to go to camp, or they earn their way by memorizing Scripture. We hire

neighbors to do odd jobs so that their wages can purchase the food, heating oil or shelter they need.

Except in dire emergencies we sell used clothing for small amounts, often as little as 10 cents an item. This allows the customers to look us in the eye as they leave. Their dignity is intact. They bought their clothes, and avoided being a charity case.

b. No loans

If there is an emergency, we give joyfully and generously. Nothing destroys a relationship like a loan.

When Bonita asked to borrow some money to buy milk for her baby, we bought milk for her instead. We explained that God was concerned about her child and through the generosity of His people He had enabled us to meet her needs. We made sure Bonita knew she did not need to repay us. It was a gift from God.

Giving, instead of loaning, helped Bonita have a positive view of God's love. It also secured a good ongoing relationship between us. Bonita had no need to be ashamed because she could not repay us. She had no reason to avoid us for fear we would demand repayment.

When we give freely, but responsibly, the recipient's

gratitude leads him to give to others, rather than to demand and expect more.

We met Brenda when her son, Steve, joined one of our Bible clubs. He wanted her to meet his Bible teachers. Brenda was grateful for our investment in Steve's life and thanked us for our impact on her community.

Raising eight children alone was quite a challenge for Brenda. We gave her food and clothes, fixed her car and cleaned her basement when her sewer overflowed. When faulty electrical work threatened to destroy her house we repaired the wiring. We involved her sons in these projects, giving them practical training and instilling in them a sense of responsibility and accomplishment as we met their mother's needs.

Each time God met Brenda's needs, her thankfulness resulted in a deeper commitment to somehow help others who had no one to provide for them. She lived for that day. Her long-standing dream came true when she was able to buy Easter outfits for two teenage girls whose mothers had abandoned them.

SELF-SUFFICIENCY

The ultimate goal of responsible giving is to help others secure a permanent solution to their problem. The adage, "Give a man a fish and he will eat for a day; teach him how to fish and he will eat for a lifetime," captures both parts of our philosophy of appropriately responding to our neighbors' needs.

We provide the tools, training and opportunities necessary to enable our inner-city disciples to successfully function as mature Christians. We offer budget counseling to stimulate good stewardship when we give emergency food, clothing or medicine. We foster self-sufficiency through education, vocational training, employment and a cooperative housing program.

9
CHRISTIAN ELEMENTARY SCHOOLS

For 17 years I watched as the majority of our Bible club students received an inadequate education. Many public schools spent more time and energy trying to maintain discipline and safety than they spent teaching reading, writing and arithmetic.

This year one of our Bible club students was wounded on her school playground by a crazed sniper. Another was shot in the head without provocation on his junior high school campus. He died a week later. The fear of being raped, beaten or robbed chokes the ability of these precious children to learn.

U.S. News and World Report (May 17, 1982) states that 44 percent of all blacks and 56 percent of all Hispanics in America are functionally illiterate. That explains why

19-year-old Randall attends a community college but scores academically at a fourth-grade level; why Allah is in the fourth grade but can only read three-letter words; why Alondra is entering the second grade but cannot count to 10, identify her colors or spell her name.

The prospect of these Bible club children becoming mature disciples of Jesus Christ and productive citizens of our country is severely diminished if they cannot read, write or verbally communicate with confidence.

God created man in His image and chose to communicate with us verbally and logically. Granted, Christians need godly character more than they need academic skills, *but* mastery of these disciplines greatly enhances their service to Christ and to others.

For over a decade the thought of providing a quality education in a Christian environment had weighed heavily on my mind. But I had more excuses than faith.

I assured our Bible club children, "I love you and God loves you," but I continued to send them off to schools plagued with violence where they had only a 50 percent chance of gaining functional literacy.

First John 3:18 says, "Let us not love with words or tongue but with actions." I was convicted of my hypocrisy. My actions had not matched my words.

Finally when three of our Bible club children were murdered at their elementary school in one week, I could dream no more.

It was no longer possible to sit back and hope that others would turn the tide or fill the void. No longer could I allow our Bible club children to go to school in fear of physical violence. No longer could I ignore the fact that they would likely never master the basic skills of reading, writing and arithmetic.

We needed a school in which Christian character, self-confidence and academic excellence could be developed in our Bible club students. These objectives would be built simultaneously. Knowledge and skill are worthless without godly character. Competence is unlikely without confidence in God, in one's God-given worth and in one's ability to learn.

A CHRISTIAN SCHOOL IN LOS ANGELES

In September, 1982 we began the Los Angeles Christian Elementary School. I wish you could have been here for our first day of classes. Our staff and constituency were so excited, I believe we had more adults standing on the sidelines—cheering, hoping, dreaming and praying—than we had children entering the classrooms.

We knew that this was one of the most significant advances that our ministry had taken.

The Los Angeles Christian Elementary School is a refreshing change from the misplaced values, pessimism and indifference usually associated with the ghetto! Our school is a beacon of God's love.

In September many of our first-grade students could not recognize or write their numbers to 20. But by June over half the class had advanced well into their second-grade math book. And every child had learned to read.

God's Word was formally taught in the classroom. The children sat entranced as we told them Bible stories. Christian principles were transmitted at every opportunity through the living curriculum of dedicated Christian teachers.

During the year our students learned 32 Bible verses and their references—and they could sing them all! Sometimes they even sang their Bible verses to correct each other after a disagreement.

We taught our students to honor and respect their parents and those in authority over them. They learned an ethical life-style, free from cheating, lying, stealing and fighting. They were encouraged to obey God by helping

At the Los Angeles Christian Elementary School, a pupil enjoys personal attention from the teacher.

Quality education in a safe Christian environment is provided children in our multi-purpose center.

their friends and neighbors and by telling them about Jesus.

Each parent paid $25 a month for his child's tuition. This was a great sacrifice for parents living on limited incomes. Those who were unable to pay worked at the school instead.

The parents' support for the school was overwhelming. We had been told that inner-city parents rarely attend parent-teacher conferences, but we had almost 100 percent attendance at each of our three conferences.

We had heard that inner-city parents would not come for school programs, yet close to 200 people came to ours. Some parents were delighted that their children had become more polite and well-mannered. Others had been touched by their children's mealtime prayers.

Robert's father expressed amazement that God was noticeably changing his son's behavior. He spread the news and now has many friends and relatives who want their children to come to our school.

Tony's "dad" told us that his son was so excited about school that he insisted on doing his homework before he would play. Minnie's mother began learning to speak English so she could be a better help to her daughter at home.

All of our students grew in character, confidence and competence.

A SISTER SCHOOL IN NEWARK

Our first year at the Los Angeles school was so successful that we began to pray about starting a sister school in Newark, New Jersey.

Newark's school system had recently vacated a vocational training school six blocks from our Youth Center. But we figured the price would be out of reach. The original cost of construction in 1922 had been $2.2 million and its replacement cost today was $15 million.

But we decided to look anyway. The school had every facility we needed:

- a full-court gymnasium, complete with a locker room and showers.
- An 800-seat auditorium, perfect for our community programs.
- Twenty-five classrooms—enough for a Christian elementary school and eventually a junior high and high school.
- A kitchen and a cafeteria.
- A library.
- Administrative offices and conference rooms.
- Space for additional staff housing.

This structurally sound, four-story building sat on 1.79 acres, right next to an interstate highway. It had a new $40,000 security system and a 75-car parking lot. And it was adjacent to concentrated housing where thousands of inner-city people needed to know about Christ's love.

It seemed too good to be true. We were almost afraid to ask the price, but after much prayer, our faith was strengthened. We pursued what, at first, had appeared to be out of reach.

We negotiated with the school district and God performed a miracle that we could hardly believe. *The school board consented to sell the property for $53,000!* And included in that price they agreed to install a new gym floor; replace all the broken windows; ensure that the electrical systems, plumbing, heating, roofs and drains were all functional; and provide World Impact with a Certificate of Occupancy for use as a school.

A few days later I mentioned this exciting possibility to a friend. He and his partner had been looking for an investment, but felt God's leading to donate the entire purchase price of this school to World Impact instead!

But that was just the beginning. Our sovereign God

Newark Christian School (top) is God's provision for the children of that city's tragic, troubled ghetto. A complete educational plant, the school contains offices, conference rooms, 25 classrooms, a full kitchen and cafeteria, auditorium (center) and a gym (bottom) with locker rooms and showers.

Vocational training at the Newark Christian School includes
auto mechanics (top) and masonry (center). A maintenance
crew (bottom) does the clean-up job.

Newark Christian School children and parents enjoy a
Christmas program in the school auditorium.

Darnell in his class at our Newark school.

was about to do more than we ever dared to ask or think.

AN ANSWER TO AN UNASKED PRAYER

Donn Norton was the president of a construction company. We had never met. The chairman of Donn's corporation had agreed to give some money to "charity" if Donn's division exceeded their financial projections. One night in September Donn signed a contract that put him over the top.

Donn was elated. Now he could channel some funds to a worthy cause. But what project would be mutually acceptable to him and his chairman? Donn simply did not know.

Soon thereafter Donn received a letter from our good friend Pat Boone which introduced Donn to World Impact. As Donn read it he felt strongly led by God's Spirit to phone us. The next day Donn visited our newly acquired school in Newark. He quickly realized that we needed his help.

The first time I toured our Newark school building I was amazed at the size of the furnaces (I probably would have fainted had I seen the utility bills at that point). Those furnaces had to be 40 feet high and 30 feet wide. And two of them sat side by side. I immediately thought about Shadrach, Meshach and Abednego. If Nebuchadnezzar would have had access to those monstrosities, well . . . .

Those two furnaces had at one time generated 25 percent of the electricity for the entire city of Newark. Apparently there were four high schools in the 1920s and each school had a similar plant.

The problem now was that cranking up those furnaces to heat that building was like using an elephant gun to kill a gnat. They heated the building all right. As a matter of fact they heated it so well you had to open most of the windows, even in the winter. And the furnaces were so big that you needed a full-time black-seal fireman (a licensed professional) to run them.

When we were considering the acquisition of this school I had sought counsel from a few experts. They assured me that we could make the building reasonably energy efficient with a $38,000 investment, enough to purchase one new furnace. That was the number I presented to our Board for approval and that was what we budgeted.

Now, I am by nature optimistic. Usually that is good. But here is a case where optimism was about to be replaced by reality.

Donn Norton brought his architects and engineers to the school. Rather apologetically they suggested that the cost to make this school energy efficient would be eight or nine times more than my estimate.

Reality was mocking my faith. But God was not to be ridiculed.

Donn's company adopted this project and made our school energy efficient. They put in 24 new gas heaters. They insulated the windows and even built a dormitory on the fourth floor for our single men's staff. What an answer to our unasked prayer!

On September 10, 1984, we opened the Newark Christian School!

"I AIN'T NOBODY'S BROTHER NO MORE"

One of our first students that September was Darnell. He had faithfully attended Bible club the previous year, but had shared little about his family. One day when he was five, Darnell quietly approached his Bible club teacher. He looked up with tears in his big brown eyes and hesitantly whispered, "I ain't nobody's brother no more."

After receiving a hug and an assurance of our love, Darnell wandered back into the crowd of children at Bible club. But what had he meant? We sought to find out.

Darnell's neighborhood looks as though it has been bombed. Burned-out buildings line crumbling sidewalks and debris-covered lots. Taverns, liquor stores and junk dealers are the only businesses left on the two-block strip called "The Market."

Day and night "The Market" is littered with staggering figures dressed in rags. Women with heavily made-up faces cluster on the corners and boldly dressed pimps cruise in their shining Cadillacs.

Darnell is the third of four children. His young mother, Sheila, has lived most of her life on "The Market." Drugs, loose sex and the horrors of murder or death by overdose were part of Sheila's life by the time she was 12. She dropped out of high school because it seemed irrelevant to her survival.

As a teenager, Sheila gave birth to one illegitimate baby after another. Sheila's alcoholic mother raised Sheila's first two children, Tamara and Felicia. But when Darnell was a toddler, the children watched as their 50-year-old grandmother drank herself to death. With the passing of Sheila's mother, what little security and stability the children had died, too.

Tamara, who was seven, kept Felicia and Darnell alive. When Abdul was born two years later Tamara and Felicia cared for him and Darnell. The girls missed entire years of school.

Sheila continued to prostitute, shoot heroin and party at "The Market." She was seldom home. The children attended Bible club and we visited them many times. Tamara was always afraid to open the door. She realized she was easy prey for the men in her building who knew the children were often left alone for days at a time.

When the temperatures plummeted, Diane, one of our Bible club mothers, found all four children staring out the grimy, cracked windows. They had been alone for over

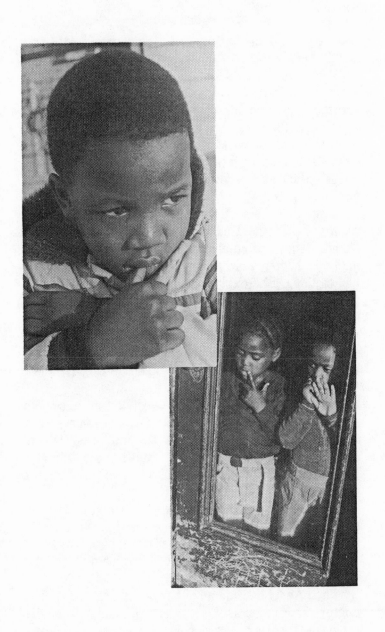

two weeks. No one had brought them food. They had no heat.

When Diane told us about this obscenity we were shocked. We had known that the children were poor. We knew that their mother was less than perfect. But we had no idea that they had been victims of such blatant neglect.

Diane took Sheila's four children to her tiny house, where she lived with her three children. A week later Sheila's place burned down. Thank God her children were no longer there.

Diane and the seven children struggled through the winter without heat except from the gas stove in the kitchen. They had no electricity. One night Diane waited until the children were asleep and then asked us for food and clothing. She explained, "They feel bad enough. I don't want them to hear me say I can't afford them."

Sheila never visited. She provided nothing for her children.

Five-year-old Darnell never smiled or cried. Anger, hurt and frustration were bottled up inside him. He knew that his mother had rejected him.

One day nine-year-old Tamara said, "I want to be with my mother, but since she won't let me, I'm gonna go live with my grandparents in Georgia. I'm tired of taking care of my sister and brothers. I just want to be a little girl. Maybe they would even get me a bike." Her grandparents consented, so Tamara moved to Georgia.

Then Felicia's father's mother took her to Pennsylvania. Felicia's grandmother wanted nothing to do with Sheila, and would not allow Darnell or Abdul to visit.

Darnell was depressed. He had lost his mother. And now his sisters were gone.

Then Abdul became so ill he was unable to eat. The doctors had never seen such severe malnutrition. He could not properly ingest vitamins. He was close to death.

The physicians assured Diane, who was guilt-ridden,

that she had not caused Abdul's plight. The damage had been inflicted through constant neglect when he was an infant. Abdul had suffered permanent brain damage from vitamin deficiency and was placed in a home where his special needs could be met.

And with that Darnell lost the very last member of his family. It was the next day that he had come to Bible club and wept, "I ain't nobody's brother no more."

A Father for the Fatherless

It would take a miracle for Darnell to become healthy and whole after such a blighted beginning. But God is "a father to the fatherless" (Ps. 68:5) and through His children God was watching out for Darnell.

I visited Darnell's class at the Newark Christian School a week after it opened. The students wore smartly tailored uniforms. Darnell was so proud of his slacks, shirt, tie and coat that he almost burst his buttons.

I asked Darnell who had tied his tie. That had always been an arduous task for me. He responded with a twinkle in his eye, "It's simple! Anyone can do it." Then he confidently reached under his collar and unsnapped the tie.

Darnell's teacher, Marcy Bullmaster, asked him to recite his memory verse for me. Darnell stood up, squared his shoulders and quoted it word-perfect. He was proud. I was even prouder.

Darnell still devours as much as he can whenever he eats with our missionaries or gets a snack in Bible club. He never refuses food because he knows what it means to be hungry. He knows many things too well for a kindergartner.

Darnell Belongs

When Darnell said, "I ain't nobody's brother no more," it was true. But it is no longer true. Today Darnell has thousands of Christian brothers and sisters across this country. And because we have the same great God and Father, Darnell is no longer alone. He belongs and we will be sure he receives God's best!

* * *

We are praying that Christian schools will be established in every city where we minister. Combined with our Bible clubs and missionaries living in the community, we then become the greatest influence on these children's lives. And we will unashamedly influence them to live for Christ.

10
TUTORING

Not every Bible club student is able to enroll in one of our Christian elementary schools. We simply do not have sufficient teachers or classrooms. And some youngsters are too old to attend our schools. We help these young people gain the academic skills they need by tutoring them.

I got to know Juanita in 1974. Her mother, Yvonne, was seriously ill, confined to bed. Her father had gone to Mexico. Juanita and her brothers and sisters had not eaten for three days.

When we brought food for this poverty-stricken family, we discovered that the children's bedroom was bare except for one filthy mattress on which all six of them slept. So we returned with new mattresses. Since the youngsters had no shoes, we traced their feet on sheets of paper and bought them each a brand new pair of shoes.

The children were ecstatic.

Six-year-old Juanita was in Ann Becker's Bible club. Two years later Juanita accepted Christ. How she loved Jesus and Ann!

LEARNING

As Ann got to know Juanita better, Ann recognized that Juanita was having serious trouble keeping up with her school work. In the fourth grade she could read only 15 words, so Ann began to tutor Juanita. The first sentence she wrote on her own was, "I am going to read and God help me to read."

Tutoring significantly deepened Ann's friendship with Juanita, a relationship which would become more and more important to Juanita as she grew older.

Ann rewarded Juanita with her first trip to Disneyland when she learned 100 words. They returned from their special day to find Juanita's house empty. While waiting for the family to come home, they received a call from Juanita's father, Manny. He threatened to kill Juanita if she did not immediately find a certain piece of paper that he needed. Manny seldom made idle threats. Juanita was scared to death.

While Manny waited on the phone Ann lovingly held Juanita. Juanita's little body shook as she explained her predicament and emphasized that she had no idea where to look for this paper. Wisely Ann suggested that they stop and pray. Juanita smiled. They asked God to show them where this paper was, and He did! Juanita was delighted.

Unfortunately that did not end Juanita's problems. She would lay awake at nights listening to her father mercilessly beat her mother. The screaming and crying were often too much for Juanita to handle. She would weep in terror and despair as she heard her mother wail.

Sometimes Juanita would intervene. But whenever she did, she ended up getting beaten herself.

At 3:00 A.M. one morning Juanita was trying to pretend that her mother's screaming and the violent breaking of dishes were merely a bad dream. Finally Juanita could take it no more.

Juanita relates, "I went into the room where my parents were yelling at each other. Dad was beating Mom again. I began to pray out loud that God would help them. That made my father furious. He grabbed my hair and threw me to the ground."

When Manny beat Juanita, she prayed for him. How she wished he would accept Christ and act like a godly father.

Juanita's mother did report Manny's abuse to the authorities, but Manny never stayed in jail for long. Though he always returned home promising to have changed, the cycle was predictable. Within a week he would start drinking and the violent fits would begin all over again.

I am so glad that Ann gave Juanita breaks from this wretchedness. Ann's presence in the midst of crisis was the only sure thing to which Juanita could cling.

Last year Juanita's plight got even worse. Her mother started drinking and began beating Juanita for no reason— just like her father did. Juanita wanted to run away. She yearned to live with Ann.

Ann listened, prayed and then counseled Juanita. Ann's gut instinct was to report this abuse to the authorities. But she had learned the hard way that if she did, Juanita would likely be taken into protective custody for a few days and then would be returned to her mother. Humiliated and embarrassed, her mother would probably inflict even greater abuse on her child. And Juanita would be worse off than if we had done nothing.

FORGIVING

For all its good intentions the legal system is inferior to God's way. Ann explained that Juanita had to forgive her mother. Juanita said that she had, but that her feelings were still hurt—understandable for a 15-year-old.

Ann read Romans 12:19-21 to Juanita and challenged her to not simply forgive her mother, but to go the extra mile and return good for evil.

Juanita left for home promising she would do what Jesus wanted her to do. The next day Juanita told Ann with a big grin, "Everything is much better now. I bought Mom a present and told her that I loved her. She was shocked!"

Ann kept tutoring Juanita. Learning became fun and Juanita felt successful. She discovered that step by step she could attain her goals if she kept at it. She became highly motivated to work hard and to do her best.

ACHIEVING

When Juanita was in the tenth grade her report card had two *A*'s, one *B* and two *C*'s—quite an improvement from age 10, when she did not know 15 words. She now reads well. And Juanita wants to be a Bible club teacher like Ann, helping children the way Ann helped her.

God's great faithfulness stands in stark contrast to the unfaithfulness of Juanita's parents. God has been with Juanita continually and has kept Christians close to her over the past 10 years.

Our Christian elementary schools foster Christlike character, self-confidence and academic excellence. Our tutoring assists others in achieving their academic potential. Our goal is to produce well-educated, capable, loving disciples of Christ no matter how long it takes. There is no quick fix.

Tutoring provides extra help for children who are having trouble keeping up with school work while also strengthening student-teacher relationships.

World Impact's Christian Leadership Training Center is located on a 560-acre Kansas ranch. A two-year program for high school graduates builds character, instills discipline and equips youths for ministry.

11

VOCATIONAL TRAINING

Working is almost second nature to me. As a child I did chores at home, odd jobs in the neighborhood and special projects at my dad's office. I watched my father work faithfully. After his death my mother worked. No one ever told me I had to work. It was assumed, part of the natural course of events.

The first biblical account of God (Gen. 1:1) describes Him as a working God: "In the beginning God *created* . . . . " He worked. And God, the Worker, created man in His image. God Himself ordained: "Six days you shall labor" (Exod. 20:9). No option. It was a simple statement of fact. If a person does not work, Scripture prescribes a harsh response: "Neither should he eat" (2 Thess. 3:10, *KJV*).

UNEMPLOYABLE

James was one of the first guys I led to Christ in the inner city. He was an unemployed, 17-year-old high school dropout. He desperately needed a job. Idle time would pull him back to the streets.

I persuaded the manager of a restaurant to give James a break and hire him as a busboy. I left feeling good.

About two hours later James came walking into the center where I was about to begin a children's Bible club. Needless to say, I was surprised. James was supposed to have been at work for another six hours.

"What happened?" I asked.

James lowered his head as he mumbled, "That manager didn't like me. He bossed me around: 'Clean this table. Pick up that glass. Don't drop the dishes.' I just couldn't take it. So I hit him in the face and knocked out one of his teeth. He fired me."

I did not understand. Why couldn't James simply do what his boss had asked? His requests seemed reasonable.

But James was not accustomed to taking orders. On the streets a guy would get worked over if he automatically did everything he was told.

Like so many of his peers, James was unemployable. He had never earned a dollar in his life. He'd had no paper route, no yard work, no experience. He'd never even had responsibilities in his home like cleaning his room, washing the dishes or taking out the garbage.

I am not defending James's actions. But I should have known that 17 years worth of bad habits could not be broken in two hours.

The skills that many of us acquired as children are often missing in inner-city teenagers. When they are young they want to work but cannot find employment because of minimum-wage laws and child-labor laws. Discouragingly, by the time they have finished high school only a handful have learned to be prompt, dependable, thorough or courteous. Few get jobs. Many join the tragic ranks of the 40- and 50-year-old men who have never worked a day in their lives.

Our teenagers come from single-parent homes. They have never seen a father who went to work on a regular basis. They do not understand why they should show up for work every day, let alone be on time. They only went to school when they felt like it. Many had no one at home who cared.

Due to the street mentality of having to be "tough" in order to survive, they find it hard to do what they are told by their boss unless they really respect him first.

Linda is a classic example.

To say that Linda had a poor home life would be an understatement. It was abominable. Linda was molested as a pre-schooler, and in elementary school she was abandoned by her parents.

When Linda did go to school, she did poorly. She didn't care. She was tough: "I don't need that stuff. I can make it on my own!"

Linda floated through her high-school years, but suddenly the day of reckoning came. Reality struck. Linda had a high-school diploma in her pocket, but that and 25 cents would barely buy her a cup of coffee.

That summer I felt strongly that it would add to Linda's self-esteem and dignity to be employed. So we hired her to work in our office.

As we do with all teenagers we hire, we took Linda through a course on the biblical basis for work. We taught her to be on time, responsible, efficient and honest. We indicated that if these qualities were not present, she would not be either. Our goal was to train Linda to become employable.

Linda did a reasonable job at her assigned task, but she

had a hard time relating to others. Soon she began missing days of work. We were forced to let her go.

There was a rapid decline after that. Linda had failed again and did not want to see us. She wanted to blame us, but somehow knew that she was the one who had blown it. When she did come to a worship service or a Bible study she looked like she had just sucked a lemon: no joy, no peace, no hope.

One day Linda said, "I'm never going to get a job. I don't even know how to talk to employers. I talk to them like street guys."

When I heard this, I knew I had to try one more time. So I asked to meet with Linda and her Bible teacher.

In our meeting it became clear to all of us that Linda needed to earn money so she would feel good about herself and so she could get an apartment away from the negative influence of her family. A regular job would alleviate the temptation of hanging out with the wrong friends and participating in unwholesome activities.

Linda thought she might be qualified to baby-sit, cook or wash cars. She admitted she could not read or write well. I asked Linda how much change I would receive if I gave her $5 and ordered a hamburger for $1, fries for 75 cents and a coke for 50 cents.

I gave Linda paper and pencil to assist her in calculating my change. At first she shook her head, as though it was too hard. Finally, after about five minutes, she responded, "$2.58."

Linda needed work on her math.

Suddenly the superficial arrogance Linda had acquired on the streets disappeared. Discouragement was written all over her face. "I can't do nothin'," she said. "I'm just gonna give up."

We talked for at least another hour. I told Linda she probably never would amount to anything unless she really wanted to. She had to be willing to do whatever it would take to make it. I told her I believed in her, but it was time for her to be realistic about who she was and what she could and could not do, and then take steps to improve herself. I promised I would help her, if she would help herself.

A smile tried to emerge. Cautiously, Linda said, "You're right. Let's get started."

So we drew up a one-year plan. First Linda would get a job—any job. She would work so hard that her boss could not afford to fire her. She would save her money and as soon as she could, she would get an apartment. Finally, she would enroll in night school and focus on improving her reading, writing and mathematics.

I coached Linda on how to apply for a job: "Dress properly—no jeans or sweatshirts. Stand tall and look the employer in the eye. Say, 'Yes, Sir,' and 'No, Ma'am,' and a lot of 'Thank you's. Be courteous and polite."

Then we practiced. And Linda did well! She promised to be persistent—not to get discouraged if the first 50 opportunities failed to pan out. We gave her money for bus fare and she was off.

Linda applied at several places. They all said, "No," "Wait" or "Maybe." But Linda kept trying. I was delighted.

Finally, four days later Linda was hired. I almost jumped for joy. Our whole staff celebrated this major victory. Daily we asked Linda how she was doing. She indicated that things were going along splendidly.

Three days later my secretary, Nancy, decided to have lunch where Linda worked. Nancy returned after only a few minutes. I thought to myself, "That place must really be efficient. That's the fastest lunch on record."

Unfortunately, Nancy had not eaten. Linda had just been fired for having a bad attitude.

With no money, no home and no job, Linda gave up. Linda is not unique.

After 18-year-old John accepted Christ we arranged for him to work at a Christian-owned business. John's responsibility was to load and unload furniture in the shipping department.

John left for work on time every morning and always came home tired. This guy who had played basketball for two or three hours every day now returned from work, ate dinner and went straight to bed.

But John lasted only three days. And he could not figure out why he had been fired. I can still hear his words, "I never worked harder in my life. I did everything they asked me to. I was always on time and never missed a day of work."

We knew the owner of the company so we went to talk with him. Since his office was in the main building he had never seen John, but phoned John's foreman to find out what had happened.

The foreman's account was revealing. John had shown up every day on time but that was where his dependability stopped. John would take one load off a truck and then sit down to rest for half an hour. Meanwhile the other men took off six more loads.

Prompted by the complaints of the other workers, the foreman had to let John go. He was too unproductive. He was there, but was hardly working.

The most hazardous time for many inner-city Christians is immediately following high-school graduation. Some of our teenagers have secured jobs or gone to college. But a large percentage have suddenly found themselves confronted with a dead end. High school was behind them; college or employment was out of reach.

Most had attended Bible club for years. They wanted to be solid Christians and productive members of society, but were virtually unemployable.

Yet without a job or further education these young believers soon lost their self-respect and much of their motivation to follow Christ. They began to believe they were worthless. Frequently, years of our loving investment in them would be lost—often within two or three months.

It seemed there was no alternative to the boredom of the streets which frequently led to drugs, alcohol, sex or violence. We had to do something to break this vicious cycle.

A BRIDGE TO THE FUTURE

In 1981 we founded our Christian Leadership Training Center on a 560-acre Kansas ranch. This two-year program for high school graduates from our Bible clubs was to become a bridge to the future.

The Training Center has three purposes:

1. *To build Christian character* through the study of God's Word and through an intensive life-on-life encounter with mature believers.

2. *To instill discipline* through hard physical work. A highly structured schedule teaches responsibility and good work habits.

3. *To equip inner-city Christians for ministry* in urban America through an intensive two-year Bible curriculum and practical spiritual leadership of others.

Reggie, who attended our first Bible club in Newark in 1976, is enrolled at our Training Center.

When Reggie was 10 years old, his mother abandoned him, his three brothers and two sisters. Reggie, the youngest child, was devastated. He waited up all night, but she never returned. From then on he saw her about once every two years. To this day he does not understand why she left.

When Reggie was 13 his brothers and sisters all moved into the streets. They drifted through the neighborhood, eating whatever they could find and sleeping in

Hard at work at the ranch, one young man tills the ground while another tackles freshly quartered logs.

condemned buildings. Reggie lived alone with his alcoholic father, Harold. When Harold was drunk he often beat Reggie.

Reggie's unmarried sister, Alice, began leaving her infant son for days at a time with Reggie and his father. Reggie nearly failed seventh grade because he stayed home so frequently to baby-sit.

Constant baby-sitting also forced Reggie to miss many teen Bible studies, so Tim, Reggie's Bible teacher, began leading a study at Reggie's house. Tim prayed with Reggie and encouraged him to obey God even during hard times. Reggie was a friendly, enthusiastic Christian with a strong desire to be God's man.

When Reggie's father lost his job they went hungry for days near the end of each month. Even worse, when they got food, Reggie's brothers broke into the apartment and stole as much as they could find. Reggie and his father often went without electricity, running water and heat. When it got real cold Reggie would huddle around someone's stove or "just keep movin'."

When Reggie was 15 his sister Alice permanently abandoned her two-year-old son and one-month-old daughter, refusing even to give Reggie her address. For three years Reggie and his father struggled against huge odds to care for these little children.

Finally Harold asked us for food. "I wouldn't take it if it was just for me. But these kids got to eat," he explained.

After Reggie's older brother Frank was released from the state prison he was stabbed in a street fight. Harold refused to help Frank since he had frequently fought with Harold and robbed him. Frank was infuriated. A bitter argument ended in serious threats.

Harold decided to get help. He locked the apartment and ran down the street to phone the police. As soon as Harold was out of sight, Frank broke down the apartment door, took the two little children out and started a fire. It gutted the entire building and left six families homeless.

Reggie, his father and the two infants moved in with a sister. But living in a tiny four-room apartment with 12 people was unbearable, so two weeks later they moved back into the burned-out building. It had no roof, no windows—and it was winter. Harold got the gas turned on and hooked up a small gas burner. The open flame was their only source of heat.

Reggie cared for the youngsters while we helped Harold search for another apartment. But the housing shortage in Newark was an insurmountable obstacle.

By this time Reggie was 17 and he could take no more. He left home, began running the streets and avoided us.

After a year on the streets Reggie recommitted his life to the Lord. He moved in with our single men's staff for the summer while he volunteered his time to help us renovate the Newark school building. Then Reggie went to our Christian Leadership Training Center.

What a change from Newark!

When Reggie arrived, the guys at the ranch were just completing the construction of five houses that they had built from scratch. He was impressed.

Roger, one of the ranch participants, asked Reggie if he wanted to see Roger's "investment." He proudly walked Reggie out to the pasture and pointed at the cows.

"I don't see any 'investment,'" Reggie protested.

"You sure do. That brown cow over there is mine," Roger insisted. "I bought it when it was a calf. The cow is my responsibility. I water it, feed it and vaccinate it. If the cow dies I lose my investment. But if it lives, when I graduate, I'll sell it and take home the profits. It's not easy. I have to care for it every day. But it's worth it," Roger explained.

Reggie was intrigued.

That first night Reggie had a hard time sleeping. It was so dark. And so quiet! No sirens. No gunshots. No noise.

We put Reggie right to work. Before long he was learning about a disciplined life-style that would radically affect his future.

Reggie learned to plan ahead. Cutting wood in 100°+ temperatures did not seem reasonable until he felt the warm fire when it snowed that winter.

Reggie learned to be thorough. If he failed to properly cultivate, plant, water or weed his garden he would have nothing to eat. He had to faithfully do each step well.

Reggie learned to be determined. Laboring in hot, humid weather drained his energy. After working all morning he was exhausted, but he learned to work hard in the afternoon in spite of how he felt.

While Reggie was at our Training Center he received a letter from his mother. He had not heard from her in years. One thing that the letter included was his full name. He had never known it before because no one had told him.

Reggie's mother also shared about brothers and sisters he did not even know he had. The most touching part of the letter was his mother's statement, "I love you, Reggie." He no longer cared why she left. He was content to know that she loved him.

Reggie's character is being built through practical, everyday experiences. He is being trained to walk with the Lord and to minister to others. Reggie promises to be a great testimony for Christ when he graduates.

PRACTICAL TRAINING FOR STUDENTS

It is extremely hard to train people to work if they have been unemployed for years. Unemployment leads to profound apathy. People demoralized by welfare expect to be given things for nothing. This erodes their incentive to seek work or to develop the necessary disciplines to maintain employment. Frequently, initiative and self-discipline

At the ranch, young men perfect their construction skills. While three carpenters work on a building another worker wheels in a barrow of fresh mortar.

have been replaced by irresponsibility and dependence.

Some people receive more money from welfare than they would earn by working. Others' welfare benefits would be reduced if they earned *any* money. We have offered jobs to several adults who could not "afford" to work.

On the other hand most teenagers will gladly work to earn money. They will sell fruit, wash cars or chop wood. And the habits they form will carry through to adulthood. Being able to spend money that they have earned is a tremendous boast to their self-worth and dignity.

Consequently we hire as many of our Christian teenagers as we can. They work for us while they are still in school. And the results have been exciting.

Liddy was one teenager who desperately needed a job.

Liddy's father began molesting her when she was 13. Every time he approached her she would cry and shake with fear. That made him furious. He could not understand why Liddy would not want him to have sex with her. He felt put down and threatened to kill Liddy if she did not loosen up.

Liddy's mother said, "It ain't no big thing. He don't mean nothin' by it. I'll buy you birth control pills."

Then Liddy became a Christian at one of our teen Bible studies. She learned that her father's sexual advances displeased God. She was thankful. She had begun to think there was something wrong with her since no one else in her family cared what her father did to her.

Liddy's sisters have several illegitimate children. One of her nieces is the child of her brother and sister. Her family thinks that is funny because the parents were high on drugs when the baby was conceived. Liddy's own brother and cousin tried to rape her.

Liddy's father printed and sold profiles on men and women. These inevitably led to sexual encounters. He made Liddy type and mail these profiles.

Liddy hated this kind of work, but most of all she hated her father. She felt guilty when a friend murdered his step-father, because she wished she could have done the same thing to her father.

Liddy desperately wanted to stop working for her father, but she needed the money for clothes, shoes and food. She had no alternative until we provided an after-school secretarial job for her. She was ecstatic!

When Liddy told her father that she no longer needed his money, he was furious at us. He told her he would kill one of us. He did come by our office with a gun once but she met him outside and talked him out of using it.

Liddy began to avoid her father at all costs. He was fit to be tied. He stopped supporting his family financially, accusing Liddy of "disrespect." The family resented her being different and mocked her faith in God.

Last year Liddy's father died of a heart attack. She was relieved. No more sexual abuse. No more threats on her life. But she also felt sad and guilty. She had completely avoided him for the last four months of his life.

After Liddy's father died, her family discovered that he had another wife in Los Angeles, plus a grown family on the East Coast. They found out his real name—he had lied to them all those years—and learned he was 10 years older than he had told them.

Liddy continues to eagerly obey God. She says, "My family and friends judge Jesus by my actions and words. I want my life to show Jesus to them."

Liddy began a Bible club for children in her apartment. She called the club, "Liddy's Impact." She also befriended a mentally slow teenager who was often ridiculed by other teens. Liddy even paid the girl's way to a bowling party.

This year Liddy supervises the playground after our Los Angeles elementary school dismisses. One mother could not afford to pay for Liddy's services in addition to the school tuition. But the mother would lose her job if her child couldn't stay. Liddy joyfully volunteered to keep the child without charge. She understood the biblical principle, "Freely you have received, freely give" (Matt. 10:8).

I am proud of Liddy. Her employment has raised her self-esteem to a level at which she now is giving to others.

A JOB FOR EVERY TEENAGER

Initially most of our employment opportunities for teenagers were limited to office work or property maintenance. Even those were sporadic.

Yet we believed that *all* of our teens needed to acquire the discipline which could come only through regular employment. They had to have a constructive outlet for their energies after school and on weekends. They needed to earn money to build their self-esteem—to buy clothes and school supplies, and to help with their families' needs.

We decided to begin businesses in each of our city ministries so that every junior high, senior high and college-age Bible club student could work on weekends or after school.

We began in Los Angeles with the Sonshine Shoppe, a thrift store run by our Christian teenagers. Young people also do our school maintenance, are in charge of after-school child care and serve as teachers' aides.

We are now challenging businessmen to sub-contract repetitive and easily measurable tasks to us so we can hire and train more teenagers to work. If teenagers can learn to be prompt, dependable, thorough and courteous while they are still in school, they will be well on their way to gaining and maintaining employment when they graduate.

Vocationally, we teach God's view of work to every Bible club student. Our Christian Leadership Training Center instills discipline and imparts marketable skills to high-school graduates. Practical training and employment opportunities for junior and senior high school and college-age youth provide valuable experience and confidence for their future vocations. These long-term strategies are building self-confident, employable disciples of Christ for urban America.

The Sonshine Shoppe, a thrift shop run by young Christians, provides job experience and earnings for eager participants (top). Trainees find that cleaning up afterwards can be part of a job, too.

12
HOUSING

God has kept the homeless poor very much on my heart. It is one thing to read the soaring statistics. It is quite another to meet those statistics face-to-face and to know the tragedy behind each number. It hurts when those faceless numbers become my friends—many of them sweet, beautiful children.

A TRAGIC NEED

When we gave our Bible club children a questionnaire to fill out, 10-year-old Leroy had a puzzled look on his face. "What should I put for my address?" he asked.

Leroy lived in four different homes. One was a hotel of disrepute next to a sleazy bar. Leroy was shuttled from one house to another, never knowing where he was going to spend the night.

And then there was Freddie, a bright eight-year-old. He had an address, but hardly a home. His mother and four brothers and sisters lived in a four-story apartment around the corner from our center.

The front door of their building had been broken off. Dozens of drunken, homeless men used the hallways for bedrooms and toilet facilities; junkies used them as "shooting galleries."

Raw sewage, backed up in the basement, caused such a stench that Freddie would gag whenever he walked out of his apartment. No one would fix the sewer because it was in the basement where the corpse of a murdered man had been found.

Freddie's mother, Debbie, kept a baseball bat by her front door to fend off intruders. One man had barged into her apartment demanding to have sex with her daughter. Debbie had to hit him in the head with a hammer to make him leave. He fled bleeding and cursing.

It was winter and there was no electricity in the building. Freddie's family wore all the sweaters, coats and gloves they owned inside their dark apartment. They huddled around an open gas flame on the stove for warmth.

One family after another fled from the tenement as the temperatures dropped and the snow built up. But Freddie's mother could not find another place that would accept that many children. Finally only three single mothers and 15 young children were left. All of these little ones attended our Bible clubs.

We were unaware of this situation until Freddie came over late one evening and politely asked to borrow candles and a flashlight. We returned home with him. Freddie's mother was shocked that we had climbed up the three stories of dark stairwells and walked down the treacherous hallways to visit her. We were shocked that she and her family had managed to survive.

With absolutely no available housing for the homeless

in Newark, and with no relatives to take them in, Freddie's family had no place to turn.

School had been Freddie's only respite from the bitter cold. But after we visited his home, Freddie spent the nights with us. God said to bring the homeless poor into your own home (see Isa. 58:7).

It was a ludicrous scandal that Freddie had to exist in such a hell hole. Our giving him temporary shelter in the winter was like putting a Band-Aid on a cancer.

A STAGGERING CHALLENGE

But how could we provide a permanent solution?

I agonized over this tragic housing shortage for years. I brought interested Christians to Newark to survey the situation. I talked with experts about housing.

But no matter how we wrote the equation the numbers would not add up—without massive government assistance. And a Christian organization walks a shaky tightrope when it is dependent upon Uncle Sam.

We needed to do something to alleviate the suffering of the homeless poor, but had exhausted our creativity. We prayed. Three years later we were still praying but there was no answer in sight. And the homeless continued to multiply.

As if to add insult to injury, Tim Goddu, our Newark director, phoned me with yet another unanswerable question. Maurice had accepted Christ two years earlier. He was reconciled to his wife and was now a godly father for his five children. I was elated with the restoration of this family.

But Maurice had been laid off work and soon after was evicted from his apartment. Tim had found Maurice, his wife, who was seven and a half months pregnant, and his children, living in the streets. It was cold. They had no place to stay.

And we had no place to offer them. We paid for a motel for that night. But what about the next night, and the next?

A PERMANENT SOLUTION

Just as our faith was wearing thin, God put all the pieces of the puzzle together. And He did it in one month.

A corporation provided the seed money with which we agreed to acquire 12 two-family homes in Newark. These 24 units had either been abandoned or were in serious disrepair.

Then a construction company consented to hire, train and supervise unemployed inner-city residents whom we knew through our ministry to renovate these buildings, thus creating jobs.

A bank agreed to loan us $40,000 at a 6 percent fixed-interest rate for 25 years on each renovated home. That loan will pay off the construction and acquisition costs of the housing and will replenish the initial seed money. We then intend to repeat the cycle.

But the most important thing is that we will have 24 quality homes which we will rent to inner-city Christians for just enough money to service the bank loan and to pay the property tax and insurance. Each resident will receive budget counseling and property-maintenance training from World Impact missionaries.

We have acquired many of these structures. Some are being remodeled. God willing all will be ready within a year. Since these homes are close to our school, Bible club children and their families will be able to walk to class, to Bible club and to worship services.

In the near future we will have good news for Leroy, Freddie and Maurice. And we pray that this pilot project will be duplicated across America!

SECTION FOUR
PREACHING THE GOSPEL

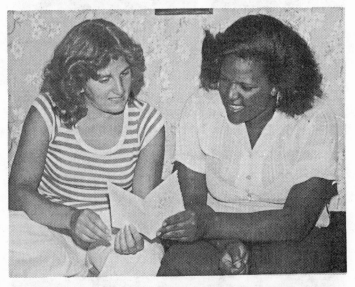

"God was reconciling the world to himself in Christ, not counting men's sins against them. And he has committed to us the message of reconciliation."

2 Corinthians 5:19

Our ministries to children take many forms: Bible clubs, craft work, story times, song fests, field trips, camping outdoors—whatever it is that will free these young people to hear and respond to the gospel of Christ. Children want to be with adults who love them for, in such adults, they see Jesus.

13
EVANGELISM

A sin-struck society, hijacked by the devil and spinning further and further away from God, would be short-changed if we merely offered a coin of social reform when we could give an inheritance of eternal life.

When Christ invaded history through Bethlehem's cradle He came preaching repentance of sins and offering eternal life for all who are born again. Those of us who bear His name must walk as He walked (see 1 John 2:6).

Because our missionaries live where they minister, an atmosphere of trust is created which frees our neighbors to hear and respond to the gospel. Anything we do that reveals the love of God to our neighbors is evangelism.

Going to the store with an elderly woman who is too afraid to go by herself, repairing the plumbing for a single mother who has neither the resources nor skills to fix it, giving food to a hungry child, providing shelter for a burned-out family: In thousands of ways, hundreds of times each day, our missionaries preach the gospel through their deeds.

Our neighbors observe and experience God's love through our life-style. But they also study the Bible and learn about Jesus in weekly Bible clubs, worship services and covenant groups.

CHILDREN'S MINISTRIES

Children were the first people to whom I ministered in Watts. I will never forget my first day 20 years ago. It must have been a strange sight, this white teenager walking through an all-black federal housing project with six eager boys trailing behind.

Within a couple of weeks, I couldn't enter the projects without scores of kids following me. I must have looked like the Pied Piper.

I have witnessed that same scene duplicated hundreds of times. As soon as our Bible club teachers arrive for club, children flock to them. Sometimes the youngsters are so excited they hardly let us get out of the car. Some are so hungry for a hug it is nearly impossible to carry our Bibles or other teaching materials.

The children love to make crafts, eat snacks, sing songs and listen to Bible stories. They are ecstatic about going on field trips or camping in God's great outdoors. They appreciate our efforts at tutoring them or helping their families with food, clothing, medicine or shelter.

But most of all these children want to be around Christian adults who love them, care about them and take time to listen to them. In these adults our Bible club children see Jesus—and they like what they see!

Through the Eyes of a Child

Teaching inner-city children about Christ certainly is a challenge, but it is a delightful challenge. One day after explaining to a group of Bible club children about the animal sacrifices that God demanded in the Old Testament, we asked the class why Abraham would kill an animal. An eight-year-old responded seriously, "Because he needed a fur coat."

In one Bible lesson we shared that after Adam and Eve sinned in the garden of Eden and recognized they were naked, God provided a skin garment for them. Then we asked the youngsters if they had ever sinned. A new child was too shy to answer, so one of our regulars looked at him and said, "You got clothes on, don't you?"

At another club we were studying the life of David. We taught that Saul had tried to kill David by throwing a spear at him. Then we asked the children what they thought might have been going through David's mind. A 12-year-old replied, "The spear."

A young girl in our Wichita Bible clubs got a little confused when she was trying to recite John 3:16. She said, "For God so loved the world that He gave His only *forgotten* Son, that whosoever believes in Him should not perish but have *terminal* life."

Some of the most memorable times for our club children happen at summer camp. Last year our staff wisely (they thought) brought their dogs along on a camping trip to make the children feel safer. During the night the dogs broke their leashes and bravely defended us against some unexpected visitors. The intruders left, but the dogs plus a good number of the campers smelled quite peculiar the next morning.

Developing deep relationships with children and teaching them God's Word often results in their becoming Christians. The change in their lives is miraculous.

A Young Evangelist

Eight-year-old Charles was bitter and angry when he first came to Bible club. His poor self-image and lack of self-control led to his threatening other kids with a knife. His numerous fights resulted in suspension from school.

Charles's poor behavior reflected his home life. His young mother, Shirley, considered herself a Christian because she attended church, but she was not walking with the Lord. Shirley often whipped Charles in anger. One night he had to have nine stitches after she hit him in the head with a belt buckle.

Shirley blamed Charles for her problems and resented him for limiting her freedom. When she got mad she would tell Charles, "I hate you! You're worthless, just like all men. You're gonna end up just like those bums down at the corner liquor store. I'd be better off if you'd just leave."

Several times Shirley threatened to put Charles in a foster home because she did not want him. He often asked his Bible club teacher, "Will you adopt me if my mom gets rid of me?"

Shirley's treatment of Charles mirrored her own tragic life. For years she had been beaten frequently by her live-in boyfriend. During this time he had several other girlfriends, but no job. Though he lived off Shirley, he called Charles "lazy" and "good for nothing." Charles resented Shirley's boyfriend's verbal abuse, complaining, "He's not even my father."

But Charles was also afraid for his mother. One night Shirley's boyfriend beat her severely. Charles called the police and then ran over a mile to find his Bible teacher. In tears, Charles gasped, "Mom needs help. She's getting beat up again. Please help!"

Tragedy and irony: An abused child was pleading for us to protect his mother from the same thing she did to him.

Ministering to an unwanted and abused child can be discouraging. Sometimes the biblical principles seem irrelevant. But they do work. The gospel is still the power of God unto salvation.

After a while Charles accepted Christ. He was at Bible club every week. He wanted to be with us continually. Soon his anger and bitterness started to fade.

We taught and encouraged Charles to love and obey his mother. We urged him to communicate daily with God. And we provided models of Christian families and godly single adults.

Happy experiences and treasured memories are delights that many inner-city children grow up without. We seek to fill this void since we deeply love every Bible club child and view each one as a future disciple of Jesus. We try to develop wholeness through expanding their horizons as far as we can.

One summer we took Charles to the mountains for a once-in-a-lifetime camping experience. We hiked up to the base of a lookout tower perched high above the surrounding peaks. Stairs stretched up to the top of the tower which extended 100 feet above the mountain.

Many youngsters never made it to the lookout. Total fear set in. Others crawled up the 400 stairs on their hands and knees. But Charles strutted up without ever looking down. When he reached the top he believed he had accomplished the ultimate in mountain climbing.

Previously Charles had overcompensated for his insecurity by being harsh or tough with his peers. But accomplishment did a marvelous thing for Charles's self-esteem. When one of his buddies got sick at camp, Charles brought food to his tent and even gave him an extra blanket.

Good memories, special experiences—all with Christians who loved Charles. These times and many more like them deepened our relationship with him while increasing his love for God.

But the turning point came when Charles worked hard to earn his way to a special outing by redeeming aluminum cans he had collected. For the first time Charles believed in himself!

After that Charles wanted to work every day. He followed his Bible club teacher around and helped in any way he could. His teacher taught Charles various work skills and encouraged him to earn money by getting jobs in the neighborhood. He liked to mow lawns, and he worked hard.

Charles started to pray for his mom and he told her about Jesus. With a little friendly encouragement from her son, Shirley began to attend our mothers' Bible study on her street.

At first Shirley admitted only that she needed to love her children more. Then after viewing the James Dobson film series at our school, she confessed she had abused Charles and she made a commitment to stop. Before long she became a dedicated Christian mother and ended her illicit affair.

But old habits die hard. When a neighbor slashed two tires on Shirley's car she cursed and hollered. After that week's worship service, she was obviously convicted about her belligerent response and asked us what to do. We suggested that she claim God's forgiveness for her sinful reaction, then forgive her neighbor and do a kind deed for him.

The next week at her Bible study Shirley shared her freedom from guilt. She had bought a treat for the neighbor's children. Even though the gift had been refused, Shirley had peace.

Shirley is growing in the Lord through our friendship, Bible study and worship times. God is healing the fear and trauma she has carried since childhood. Shirley prays with and ministers to other mothers. But the biggest change is in her improved relationship with her children.

It all began when Charles accepted Christ at our Bible club. Now we are ministering to his whole family. We have provided emergency food. We help Shirley do her taxes, budget her money and maintain her car. She purchases badly needed clothing and shoes at bargain prices at our Sonshine Shoppe. And she plans to enroll her four-year-old daughter at our Christian elementary school.

Few things thrill me more than seeing Shirley with her children at our worship service. That home united in Christ is a testimony to God's grace and power.

Shirley has often expressed that Charles's only chance in life began when he met our staff. She now dreams that someday he will go to our Christian Leadership Training Center and make her proud.

We will continue to love Charles as he grows up, confident that our close friendship will influence his important decisions. We will pray for the protection and divine guidance he needs to develop into a godly man.

We will teach Charles to remain pure, knowing that once a person has had an illegitimate child the entire course of his life is negatively affected. Even though nothing is impossible with God, illicit parenthood is a heavy burden to carry and diminishes the probability that someone will become a mature Christian.

When Charles becomes an adult he will be able to form a Christ-exalting family. It will take years of faithful investment to watch this dream become a reality, but that is a small price to pay for a secure, functioning disciple of Jesus Christ. And it is the most reasonable way to engender indigenous Christian leadership in the city.

MINISTRY TO TEENAGERS

Beginning relationships with inner-city children was a piece of cake compared with ministering to teenagers. The teenagers were justifiably suspicious. They had seen plenty of do-gooders come and go and had believed lots of broken promises. They had watched just as many outsid-

Ministering to teenagers is a challenge in itself. Broken promises and a high turnover of do-gooders rouse justifiable suspicions. But in time, through teen Bible clubs, varied recreational and athletic events, choir, camping and social times, barriers fell and friendships developed. As young men and women found Christ and then won others, an ongoing inner-city evangelistic ministry among youth began.

ers plunder their community. They wondered who we were and why we were there. The only white people who came to their neighborhood were undercover police, absentee landlords, con men, pimps, prostitutes or pushers.

It threw the teens off that we had actually moved into their community. They were even more puzzled when they heard kids singing religious songs and saw them carrying Bibles. But for the most part they continued to play it cool—they'd wait and see what our real motives were before they committed themselves.

Some of our staff were scared by the teens' cold, threatening stares. A simple "hello" or an acknowledging nod was the most we could expect the first few months after we moved in.

We knew that our Bible club children would eventually become teens. If we were patient we could start our teen ministry with them. It is easier to build a boy than to remake a man.

Yet we could not just write off the present teenagers. They needed Christ too. But as we continued to reach out to them our initially chilly reception turned into a baptism of fire.

When Mary Thiessen first walked into the housing projects she was introduced to a group of young men by one of her new teen Bible club students. The teen shamelessly declared, as she grabbed Mary's wrist and raised her arm, "This girl's for sale!"

Soon after Kim Seebach joined our staff he found three teenagers working on a car in his backyard. One dude asked Kim for a screwdriver and a pair of pliers. Wanting to establish a good rapport with these guys Kim willingly obliged. But as Kim thought about what these guys were doing, it suddenly clicked. They were stripping the doors, fenders, chrome parts and engine off a car they had stolen. And he was helping them!

Larry faithfully attended Gary Friesen's teen Bible club. Larry also frequented Gary's house as an uninvited guest, regularly breaking in and stealing whatever he could find. Usually, after the following Bible club Larry would confess that he had robbed Gary, but would sadly report that he had already sold the merchandise and there was no way he could get it back.

One day Larry stole a $120 camera, which he fenced for $15. He said he was sorry he had stolen it and was a bit embarrassed he had sold it for so little. He hadn't realized its value.

Never one to pass up a good opportunity Larry made Gary a proposition: "I'll tell you who I sold the camera to, if you pay me five bucks. I'm sure the guy would sell it back to you for $15." Fortunately, Gary did not fall for Larry's smooth talk and at least prevented losing an additional $5.

I Wish I'd Never Had a Father

Through the years we have developed good friendships with many teenagers. When a Bible club child enters junior high school he matriculates into one of our teen Bible studies. We continue to encourage him in his Christian life and teach him about God's Word. He has regular fellowship with other inner-city believers through recreation, choir, camping, social events and corporate worship.

Our Christian teenagers frequently tell their friends about Jesus and bring them to Bible club, too. Many accept Christ and are incorporated into our ongoing ministry. Florence was such a person.

Florence's life began in tragedy. Her twin sister was born dead. Her mother, who had been abandoned as a baby herself, was living on welfare in a federal housing project in Watts. Florence was the fourth of seven children by five different fathers.

Before Florence was born, her 23-year-old father was

shot in the head and killed by a man who accused him of having an affair with his wife.

Florence recalls, "For as long as I can remember my brothers and sisters teased me because of how and why my father died. Besides that the only thing I ever knew about him was that he made his living stealing welfare checks. I wish I'd never had a father!"

When Florence's mother became a motel maid nine-year-old Michael, her eldest son, cared for the other children. Michael soon began stealing when there was not enough food. Before long all the children stole. They played cards and shot dice to "earn" money.

When Florence was six she got beat up by an eight-year-old girl. Her dress was torn, her face was swollen, her arms and legs were bruised. Florence ran into her apartment sobbing.

Michael listened intently to Florence's sad rendition of her skirmish and began to walk toward her. She could hardly wait to be held tightly and comforted by her big brother. He would protect her. No one messed with Michael.

But to Florence's dismay Michael grabbed her, pulled up her dress and burned a permanent scar into her stomach with a hot light bulb. Then he shouted, "You go back and fight that girl. You better never lose another fight."

Florence learned a lot from watching her older brothers. She learned how to fight and steal. And she learned that boyfriends and girlfriends sleep together. So she and a nine-year-old boy began to experiment sexually. She thought this was the right thing to do.

When the Watts riots broke out Florence was in the third grade. Michael brought home boxes of clothes from burned-out or abandoned stores. Florence watched the armed guards, mostly white, walk around the projects. She heard them order people, "Be in your house by 6:00 P.M. or we'll shoot your black behinds."

Florence went to a Catholic elementary school, but even there she stole, fought and smoked dope regularly. She recalls, "I always lied to the priest when I went to confession. I knew I'd be in serious trouble if anyone knew the whole truth."

Things deteriorated rapidly through junior and senior high school. Florence lost her job as a teacher's aide because she was too high to work. She was kicked out of a Catholic high school three months before her freshman year ended. But her troubles only intensified. Florence ditched public school frequently and became involved with a couple of "boyfriends."

Florence spent that summer with her mother's friend, Nancy. One Saturday a nice-looking man came over to visit Nancy. He was more than twice Florence's age. Florence noticed that he was being unusually kind to her. He smiled at her and laughed at all her jokes. Then he asked Nancy if Florence could spend the night at his house and attend church with him in the morning. Nancy agreed.

Florence packed her clothes and jumped into the car with this total stranger. He took Florence to an X-rated movie and then to his apartment. Florence was scared. She had never been with an older man. But when he gave her some wine, she relaxed and agreed to go to bed with him.

The following morning he drove Florence back to Nancy's house, but before Florence got out of the car he gave her $30 and said he hoped they could get together again. Florence was puzzled. "Why would he give me money?" she wondered, but accepted it anyway.

Several relationships with older men followed. Florence liked them because they paid her money.

Florence's life seemed hopeless. Many people would have written her off. But not God!

During Florence's junior year in high school her youngest sister started attending our Bible club. Florence had been very upset when she had first seen these white women living on her street. Michael had taught her to hate all white people and to have nothing to do with them. Florence thought her sister was a fool.

Florence watched closely for several more months, trying to discover a good reason to hate these Bible teachers. But they were just too friendly, too nice. Yet why would white girls move into the ghetto? Maybe they were using this Bible stuff as a cover for turning tricks.

Finally Florence's sister persuaded Florence to come to Bible club just once. She agreed, simply to get her sister off her back. Florence remembers, "That first night I saw something wonderfully different about these people. They had peace and joy, and a genuine concern for each other and for us. They were interested in me. They listened to me. I loved the attention. I had never had anyone to really talk to or to share my problems with. After attending that Bible club I knew that I should come every week."

And come every week she did.

At one of her first Bible clubs Florence heard a lesson on purity. Mary Thiessen, Florence's Bible teacher, explained to the class that having sex outside of marriage was wrong. Florence was shocked. At first she thought Mary was joking. But when she realized Mary was serious Florence did not know if these missionaries had been living in a monastery or had just stepped out of the Dark Ages. She had never heard anyone say that God disapproved of premarital sex.

But since all the other girls in the class were nodding their heads in agreement, Florence pretended to know what Mary was talking about. Florence nodded her head as vigorously as the rest.

Florence continued stealing, messing around with guys and smoking angel dust. But God was convicting her about her need to know Him. She felt miserable about her past and frankly did not think God would forgive her.

However, once Florence understood that Jesus' death had paid for all her sins, she accepted His free gift. Florence became a Christian on her graduation day from high school!

Florence expected her life to change immediately. But when she found it difficult to give up her old ways she got discouraged and thought being a Christian was too hard. We taught her about the power of the Holy Spirit and surrounded her with love.

Florence says, "God changed my fleshly desires so I can now live for Him. He replaced my shame and guilt with peace and joy."

Belonging is terribly important to teenagers. Our staff homes are always open and many teens "live" there without actually moving in. Florence, like so many others, became a frequent visitor at Mary's home.

Mary had grown up in a large family—10 children! Times were tough and Mary's parents had struggled to make ends meet. All the children worked on the farm.

In place of watching television, Mary's family played games, made crafts, sang songs and told a lot of jokes. Mary never realized she was poor. Nor did she know how God would use her childhood experiences to help her create a special sense of "familyness" in her home when she became a missionary.

When Florence dropped by our women's home she never knew what to expect. Sometimes she played board games, charades, basketball or volleyball. Other times she exchanged jokes, listened to Christian music, sang songs or memorized Scripture. She loved the warmth, fun and activities that Mary initiated.

And much to Florence's own surprise she even began to like doing the dishes, washing the floors and cutting the grass. The activity did not matter. It was special just being with Christians. And Florence could not get enough.

Our investment in Florence paid off. Today, over 10 years later, she is serving the Lord wholeheartedly.

ADULT MINISTRIES

Several people who started in our children's Bible clubs are now adults. What a joy it is to watch them live for God! Some have married and formed Christ-centered homes. Many participate in weekly Bible studies, covenant groups and worship services. Some have joined our staff; others volunteer in Bible clubs like the ones in which they learned about Jesus.

However, most of the adults to whom we minister are single parents. They present a special challenge.

We got to know 22-year-old Veronica through her sons, Willie and Bobby. They faithfully attended our Bible club and their younger brother could hardly wait to join. Shortly after we met Veronica she gave birth to her pride and joy, a baby girl.

But two months later crib death struck. Veronica nearly went crazy. She sobbed at the funeral as she showed us pictures of her baby. Veronica blamed herself for her infant's death.

We continued to minister to Veronica and to her family. We prayed with her and for her.

Veronica asked us to pray that Leonard, the man with whom she was living, would marry her and that they would move out of the housing projects. Her request was understandable, except that Leonard was also the father of two other children in our Bible club. They lived with their mother two blocks from Veronica.

Leonard's four-year-old son by the other woman constantly talked about wanting to live with his father again. We faced a real dilemma in Bible club when the sons of both mothers prayed that their father would move home with them.

Leonard frequently served time in prison. He was one of the main suppliers of narcotics locally. He got Veronica hooked on drugs and started her in prostitution.

As if Veronica's life were not bad enough, calamity struck again. Her son Willie was hit by a car while riding his bicycle. He received extensive brain damage, slipped into a coma and died.

The multiple tragedies began to take their toll.

Veronica kept her remaining two sons in the house away from their friends, even away from school. She was paranoid that something would happen to them. Veronica tried to kill herself by not eating and by shooting up drugs. She became deathly sick and weighed only 87 pounds.

That was when Patricia Williams began a Bible study with Veronica. It was difficult because Veronica could read only a few sight words. When she memorized one short verse she was so proud she felt like a queen.

To add to Patricia's challenge of teaching Veronica the Bible, people were buying, selling and using drugs in the same room. They did not seem one bit worried about Patricia's presence. They kept tying up their arms and shooting up. Patricia discovered that these junkies paid Veronica to use her house as a shooting gallery.

Leonard did not like Patricia filling Veronica's mind with "that junk" about being precious in God's sight. It was bad for business. Even as Patricia shared that God promised complete forgiveness for Veronica's past, men knocked at the door asking to buy Veronica's body.

Veronica understood some of the truths Patricia taught her. She wanted a better life for her sons. So she enrolled Bobby in our Christian elementary school.

One Saturday Patricia arrived to take Veronica to place flowers on Willie's grave. As they were leaving, Veronica told Leonard there was no food in the house. He had a pocketful of money but refused to help. In Patricia's presence, Veronica told him to pack up his stuff and get out.

Leonard was furious. His pride was hurt. He returned that evening and beat Veronica with a baseball bat. She screamed and begged him to stop. He broke two of her ribs before she was able to grab a knife and force him to flee.

Finally Veronica accepted Christ. But our joy was short-lived.

Veronica could not kick the drugs. She began shooting heroin into the veins in her neck. Needle tracks scarred her arms. Blood vessels broke in her swollen, puffy eyes.

Veronica's son Bobby told his teacher at our school one day, "My momma went to the hospital last night 'cuz a needle broke off in her neck."

During this time Leonard was arrested again. While he was in prison he made a profession of faith in Christ. After his release he moved Veronica and her sons out of the projects. He helped Veronica kick her habit cold turkey and made sure that Bobby attended school regularly.

It is too early to know if our ministry to Veronica will result in lasting fruit. While both Veronica and Leonard claim to have accepted Christ as their Saviour, they are not married. We are not even sure if they should marry. The open wounds from Leonard's other family are unhealed; his other children still feel rejected. We will remain faithful and do everything we can for each parent and child involved. But there is no easy answer. There is no quick fix.

The discipler and discipled, Mary Thiessen (left) and Patricia Williams, now serve Christ together.

A beautiful woman with a contagious smile—an apt description of Patricia Williams. So real is her joy in Christ that one of Patricia's most profound ministries is her presence. She teaches six Bible clubs each week, disciples two other women and does follow-up work with teens while directing a staff home. But she always finds time to hug a friend!

14
DISCIPLESHIP

Once someone accepts Jesus as his Saviour we begin the long process of Christian nurture. First we enter into a follow-up relationship in which we teach the new believer how to feed himself spiritually.

After he demonstrates a commitment to obeying Christ, we equip him to join with us in teaching others, just as Christ trained His disciples. This is discipleship.

Making disciples is the best way to build functioning, indigenous leadership for Christ in urban America. Patricia Williams is an excellent example of how discipleship works.

Patricia accepted Christ in a Bible club in Watts in 1972. Like so many youngsters to whom we minister, Patricia had grown up in a poverty-stricken home without a father. Leading Patricia to Christ was a great joy for her Bible teacher, Mary Thiessen. But teaching Patricia to live the Christian life was quite a challenge.

Christ's disciples learned how to please God by being with Christ. They watched Him minister to Jews and Gentiles, friends and enemies. They saw Christ heal the sick, feed the hungry and befriend the outcast. Before long they became His assistants, distributing the loaves and fishes and rowing the boat after He preached. Soon they were actively ministering with Him.

Christ's method of training by example and participation worked. His disciples later planted the Church and "turned the world upside down" (Acts 17:6, *KJV*) for Christ. Even their enemies attributed the disciples' success to their life-on-life encounter with the Master: they had "been with Jesus" (Acts 4:13)!

And Mary adopted Christ's method. She trained Patricia through example and participation. Patricia lived with Mary during the summers and spent most weekends with her.

Patricia shares, "Mary invested in every area of my life. I graduated from high school with good grades, but had only read one book. Mary was really the one who taught me how to read and write."

Mary studied the Bible, prayed, memorized, sang and worshiped with Patricia. Of course, Patricia was with our other missionaries a lot, too. She could not believe how much they loved each other and how they treated her. She wanted to be like them.

Patricia explains, "They all ate together, which was new for me. We had never done that in my home, but I thought it was wonderful. So I spent a whole day making dinner and setting the table for my family. When everything was finally ready, they each picked up their food off of my beautifully set table and went their separate ways. No one joined me to eat. I was heartbroken, but nobody cared."

One summer Patricia and Mary went to visit Mary's

parents. That trip to the family farm in Canada made a lasting impression. They ran in the fields, rode horses, milked cows and drove tractors. But significantly, Patricia most clearly remembers Mary's family eating together and enjoying one another.

When Patricia returned she tearfully expressed, "I had never seen a complete family in the city, where all the children had the same father and the parents have been faithful to each other. Mary's family was so different. They seemed so happy. I had no idea that a family could be like that."

Patricia learned how to teach children's Bible clubs first by watching Mary and eventually by team-teaching with her. Patricia's observation of and involvement with Mary in ministry was the most practical training we could provide for Patricia.

Now Patricia is a disciple, passing on to others what she has learned. Each week she teaches four Bible clubs for children and two Bible clubs for teenagers. She leads follow-up relationships with two teenage girls, disciples two women and directs one of our women's staff homes in Los Angeles.

Patricia is one of our best Bible club teachers. Children flock to her clubs, listen attentively and treasure the personal attention they receive from her. They know that Patricia grew up in the same community where they live. They see the love of Christ in Patricia, and they want to be like her.

MODELING

One of Patricia's most profound ministries is her presence. For years little girls in the inner city have seen only two options in life: They can have illegitimate children and start their own welfare homes; or they can become prostitutes.

Patricia presents a third option. Now children can choose to follow Jesus and live pure, godly lives. They know they can, because Patricia is doing just that.

Those of us who know Patricia's past recognize what a miracle her life is. For as long as Patricia can remember, her uncle sexually molested her. He threatened to kill her if she ever told anyone. Patricia hated herself, hated her uncle and hated all men because of her uncle's abuse.

It took Patricia four years to begin to share those hurts with Mary. But because Mary stuck with Patricia, loving and discipling her, Patricia finally believed that Jesus had paid for all her past pain. She started to receive God's healing and even forgave her uncle.

At first Patricia did not want anyone else to know that she had been sexually abused. However, she eventually realized that she needed other Christians to help carry her burden; she needed to experience the love and acceptance of believers who knew the truth about her past. Gradually God completely healed Patricia of her hurt and bitterness.

I had never seen such a remarkable transformation. I do not mean just spiritually. Patricia blossomed into a beautiful woman with the most contagious smile. God filled her with His peace and joy.

Before long Patricia began praying that God would use her to help others with similar pasts find His healing. And God answered her prayers. When Patricia shared her testimony with our teenage girls many took steps toward becoming free from the oppression of past abuse.

Belinda opened up immediately. The timing was incredible. Belinda was in the middle of court proceedings in which she was being forced to testify against her father, who had raped her. Her pain was intensified because now her mother was accusing Belinda of trying to split up her parents' marriage.

Then another teenager wept, "I've wanted to tell you for so long, but I was afraid you wouldn't love me any more. I've tried to be close to God, but every time I pray it's like there is a block between me and Him. Do you think God can help me forget about my father raping me?"

Patricia assured both girls that God could heal them. Step by step, over months and years of counseling, they accepted God's forgiveness, forgave themselves and then forgave the person who had abused them.

Patricia says, "I believe God will heal each one because He healed me. I understand and care." God will use Patricia to help many others. Her life is a testimony to the Father's complete love!

REPRODUCTION

Patricia's ministry extends past evangelism and follow-up. Just as Mary trained Patricia, Patricia is training others. One woman she is discipling is Barbara.

Barbara was born in Louisiana. When she was six months old her mother gave Barbara to her grandmother to raise. Each time Barbara's mom had another child she dropped it off at Grandma's.

Then Barbara's mother ran away to Los Angeles with a boyfriend. It was two years before Barbara found out where her mother had gone.

Strange things go through a child's mind. Barbara had never known her father, but wondered if she had caused him to leave. Maybe she had been such a difficult infant that her mom had been forced to let her grandma raise her. Maybe she had driven her mom to leave Louisiana.

Barbara never admitted these feelings to anyone. But how could she help having a poor self-image?

Barbara worked in the fields helping her grandmother pick cotton. Barbara and her sister were so poor that they went to school on alternate days because they had only one pair of shoes between them.

But the indignities of poverty were nothing when compared with the degradation of racism. The Ku Klux Klan rode through Barbara's neighborhood shooting into houses. One night they burned a cross on her front yard. She remembers, "There was nothing we could do but hide. Who would you call for help? The police? Half the officers were wearin' white sheets and hoods."

In 1968 when Barbara was 11 her mother returned and took her six children to be with her in Los Angeles. It was the biggest surprise of Barbara's life. Barbara thought, "Maybe I judged my mom too quick. Maybe she is going to do me right."

All the way to Los Angeles—and it is a *long* way from Louisiana with six children and two adults in a sedan—the kids could not stop talking about how surprised they were to be headed west.

But when they arrived in Los Angeles they discovered an even greater surprise. Their mother had three more kids. And now they were all going to live together: nine children from six different fathers in a two-bedroom apartment. And that did not include Barbara's mother and grandmother.

Barbara had "bad feelings" about her mother. Barbara started to spend every free hour she had at the park to avoid fighting with her mother. Besides it was too crowded at home.

Barbara's friends at the park became the strongest influence in her life. They introduced her to drugs when she was 12 and taught her how to steal. When Barbara felt bad about stealing they told her it wasn't wrong because she needed those things.

Barbara acted tough to overcompensate for her poor self-image. She fought almost every day at the park or at school to earn respect. She even slapped a teacher to prove she was not afraid of her.

About this time World Impact started a Bible club at Barbara's park. Barbara and her sisters and cousins decided to join. Almost immediately they all accepted Jesus. It seemed like a good thing to do.

But Barbara soon fell back into a life of drugs, gangs, drinking and sex. She only thought about God when she feared getting caught.

Eventually, to please her friends, Barbara dropped out of Bible club completely. She figured that the missionaries wouldn't last long in her neighborhood anyway. It was a better bet to stick with her friends who would always be around.

But then Barbara's tough facade began to crumble. First, her mother tried to kill herself. Barbara was shaken. She watched the ambulance take her mom away.

Then at school a gang suddenly swarmed in on Barbara and her buddies from the park. The gang shot Barbara's good friend, Antoine. He slumped down and died at her feet.

The same gang threatened to get Antoine's friends, and that meant Barbara. The principal explained that it was impossible for him to protect Barbara so she would have to transfer to another high school.

Barbara was scared. The security that she had worked so hard to build up was being stripped away. She had nowhere to run, no one to talk to. She was all alone. At times she could not stop crying. She just sobbed and sobbed.

Barbara could not even find peace when she slept. In her nightmares she would see Antoine's face when he'd been killed. At times she would see her own body in Antoine's grave. Barbara relates, "I just couldn't take it anymore. I had to get help."

Finally Barbara mustered up the courage to call her Bible club teacher whom she hadn't seen in two years. Her teacher not only listened, she invited Barbara to come over that same night. Barbara was shocked that her teacher cared at all.

That evening Barbara learned that God would forgive her for everything she had done because He really did love her.

Barbara recalls, "I made a commitment right then to do whatever God wanted. Soon Patricia Williams began to meet with me. If she hadn't given me that personal attention I never would have made it."

Patricia cared enough to invest in all areas of Barbara's life. As time went on Patricia taught Barbara the importance of staying in the city and making disciples. Patricia explained that if all those who became Christians left, the cycle of hatred, murder and drugs would never end.

Barbara has never waivered in the commitment she made following her friend's death. Eventually Barbara joined our staff. She teaches four children's Bible clubs and two teen clubs. She is discipling another woman and is following up a teenager. Barbara says, "Only God can help people have real joy and life with a purpose."

Barbara's changed life has affected her family. Barbara has forgiven her mother and has developed a close relationship with her. Barbara's mother has been very convicted by her daughter's life and has become increasingly interested in the Lord. Barbara's sister, who accepted Christ in Bible club, is also on our staff.

But Barbara's friends from the park have not followed her example. Nine have been in the mental ward of County General Hospital, one committed suicide, one was murdered by a boyfriend and two others have several illegitimate children each. The fate of Barbara's friends accentuates the miracle of God's saving grace in Barbara's life.

There is no quick fix. However, discipleship does work. Patricia and Barbara are living proof. It takes years of loving, caring investment, but discipleship is changing the ghetto!

SECTION FIVE
GOD'S URBAN RENEWAL

"'For my thoughts are not your thoughts, neither are your ways my ways,' declares the Lord. 'As the heavens are higher than the earth, so are my ways higher than your ways and my thoughts than your thoughts.'"

Isaiah 55:8,9

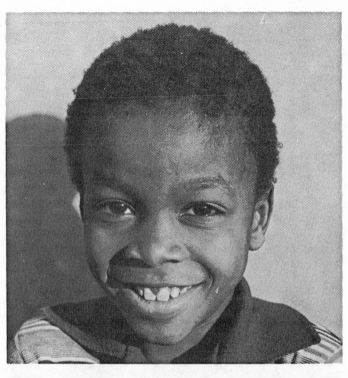

15
Man's Ways

"There ain't no quick fix."

It was not the answer I had expected, but it was the truth.

I had just asked a young addict, bent over in obvious pain, if there was anything I could do to help. He could not have been over 15. Yet his face was drawn, scarred by wrinkles far beyond his years.

He had just had a fix but he knew it wouldn't last. And he was just as sure it didn't really fix anything.

He needed help, a lot of help. He was barely hanging on to life. What a pathetic representative of a broken and defeated people!

DEPENDENCY AND DESPAIR

No one questions the fact that urban America needs a radical rebirth. The New Frontier and the Great Society sounded the hopeful notes of emancipation from poverty, degradation and second-class citizenship. But the bottom line was an increasing crime rate, escalating narcotics abuse, soaring murder statistics, additional illegitimate children, proliferating broken families and a dependence upon "big brother" for a cup of porridge.

The government treated the cancerous symptoms and wondered why the illness spread. It spent millions of dollars to build an iron lung, but not a nickel to cure the disease. We fell into the trap of giving people what they wanted, not what they needed.

Federally-funded housing does not build pride. Food stamps do not engender character. Giveaways do not restore dignity. Handouts beget greed and resentment. A faceless bureaucracy is an easy mark to rip off and manipulate without guilt.

Masses play the role of the blighted lame man depicted in Acts 3. His condition was so pathetic that others had to carry him to the place where he could beg for alms—an indignity he perceived to be the highest state to which he could aspire.

Most well-intentioned government subsidies were designed as compassionate responses to glaring needs, but inevitably these programs have destroyed the human spirit. They perpetuate a permanent underclass of God's children by stealing their dignity, pride and hope.

The ghetto stands as a crumbling memorial to the failure of secular humanism.

In order for significant lasting improvement to occur, members of an oppressed society need to experience hope, healing and justice. But without hope, healing is impossible and justice is worthless.

A person who does not like himself, believe in himself or have a vision for his future is of all people to be most pitied. One whose inner spirit has been broken, whose self-concept has been reduced to repulsion, borders on self-destruction. Hopelessness!

Street dudes ridicule anyone who attempts to break out of their futile life-style. They jeer when one of their own applies himself academically. They laugh at any friend who works.

While painting his mother's house, one teenager was mocked by a group of his friends who stood idly across the street. They fired off one salvo after another: "Man, you're really getting used." "You think you're something." "Aren't you cute?"

Finally the crowd prevailed. The youngster told his mom, "You ain't got no right to make me do that. I quit." He stopped painting and lost the pride and self-respect that were almost within grasp.

HERITAGE AND HOPE

What a contrast to individuals who are secure and loved. They experience hope in the worst of situations. Recently I visited a refugee camp in Hong Kong. A huddled mass of humanity had fled for their lives from all over Asia—poor, uprooted, but not broken. The human spirit had escaped unscathed.

The refugee children stood proudly in line before dawn to go to school. They were well prepared and better educated than many of our neighbors. After school little children worked hard with their older brothers and sisters to earn a few dollars which would help feed the family. Youngsters spoke of starting businesses, becoming professionals.

Why would two equally oppressed peoples vary so radically? The only difference I could see was that the Asian boat people and refugees *had hope.* They had the heritage of whole family units—confident, industrious models to follow. While some parents had died, the children still had fresh mental pictures of who they should become and fully intended to copy what they remembered.

By contrast our urban neighbors seldom see whole family units or healthy models after whom they can pattern their lives. The professionals, businessmen, athletes and entertainers who break out of the chains of poverty integrate into society's mainstream and live in a different world. These former poor hardly provide real-life models for those left in bondage.

Unless there is a realistic approach to restoring human dignity and pride—to injecting hope into the masses trapped in the ghetto, the cycle will repeat itself ad infinitum. There must be a dramatic rebirth of the human spirit. And this is exactly what God desires.

16
GOD'S WAYS

God's approach to renewing the cities is radically different from man's. Instead of painting bright make-up on a dead body to give the illusion of vitality, God offers to breathe a new spirit into the corpse to give it life.

Over 2,500 years ago God promised to rejuvenate a hopeless, sick and oppressed people: "They will be called oaks of righteousness, a planting of the Lord for the display of his splendor. They will rebuild the ancient ruins and restore the places long devastated; they will renew the ruined cities" (Isa. 61:3,4).

But how did God propose to fashion these redeemed citizens of a new order who would renew their ruined cities? He certainly offered no placebo, no quick fix. God realized it would take the greatest urban renewal program in history because He demanded that the people themselves must change first. The prerequisite for society's salvation was that individuals become oaks of righteousness.

And to facilitate this transformation God sent a Prophet, a Priest and a King—His own Son—to bring hope, healing and justice. This is the essence of Christianity.

If ever a society has needed to claim God's promise of rejuvenation it is the ghettos of America.

Today Christians walk in the footsteps of Christ on this weary, sin-struck planet. We have been anointed by the sovereign Lord of the universe to be His ears to hear the cries of oppression; to be His voice, His hands and His feet to respond with hope, healing and justice.

The prophetic, priestly and kingly work of Christ is ours. Through us, oaks of righteousness will be established and ruined cities will be renewed.

THE GHETTO NEEDS A PROPHET TO PREACH THE GOOD NEWS THAT IN CHRIST THE OPPRESSED CAN BE RECONCILED TO GOD

God demands that real renovation begin with an inward conversion. Repentance is a change of mind; conversion is a change of direction: turning from sin, selfishness and hatred toward the love of God. Making peace with God produces a new motivation, a new purpose, a new hope.

Fifteen-year-old Tanisha needed a prophet. She needed hope.

Even though Tanisha faithfully attended our teen club something held her back from becoming a Christian. One week Mary Thiessen taught a Bible lesson on God's mercy. After club Tanisha began crying.

Mary asked Tanisha if she wanted to accept Christ. She nodded "yes," but was so choked up she could not talk.

Mary asked Tanisha if she was afraid to become a

Christian. "No. It's something that happened two years ago," she confessed, continuing to sob as if her heart would break.

Tenderly Mary began to pray and God's Spirit quieted Tanisha. Finally she managed to explain: "My mother's boyfriend raped me at knife point when I was 13. I have a baby by him."

Then Mary declared the good news. God had healed others in Tanisha's club who also had been raped. Jesus had paid not only for her sins but also for the grief and sorrow she had experienced as a result of the sins of others. When Tanisha heard this she immediately understood the gospel. She prayed to receive Christ. Release! Freedom! Hope!

Jesus miraculously lifted Tanisha's burdens. When she got home, she bounded into her house and told her mother of her new life in Christ. Even though it was late at night, she phoned her cousin to announce the good news. The next week at teen club, Tanisha beamed as she told all 24 girls in her class what God had done. Everyone cheered! Tanisha has hope!

THE GHETTO NEEDS A PRIEST TO HEAL THE BROKENHEARTED

Just as broken bones are bound so that they may knit and close again, the gospel of Christ binds the wounds of injured people like Thelma.

When Thelma was five her mother left her in the care of her older cousins who molested her. When she was in the fifth grade her 40-year-old uncle began having sex with her. Then in elementary school both of Thelma's parents left. Her alcoholic father stayed with a girlfriend. Her mother moved in with a boyfriend.

Thelma lived with her two brothers, four sisters and their seven babies—14 people under the age of 21 in one house. Thelma slept on an old couch in the front room where her family and their friends gambled, drank and did drugs until the early hours of the morning.

When one of Thelma's sisters attempted to kill her own 14-month-old child Thelma was furious. "I was so mad, I wanted to beat my sister's brains out," she cried. "I'd take the baby away and raise it myself if I could."

Thelma remembered the abuse she had received as a child. She recalled, "My mother would wet my body and then whip me with an extension cord, or she'd tie me to the bed and snap me with a heated wire hanger. She refused to take me to a doctor when I broke my arm. That arm is still crooked."

Thelma often thought about turning herself in to the authorities so she would be placed in a foster home.

Thelma began attending Bible club while she was in the sixth grade. Two years later she accepted Christ. But she still needed to experience healing.

One time when Thelma's mother lost half her welfare check gambling she beat Thelma unmercifully, without reason. Finally the adults present begged her not to kill Thelma.

Thelma told us later, "It's not hard for me to forgive her. She's frustrated and takes it out on me. I remind her of my father and that makes her mad." Then Thelma began to cry, "Every night I dream about my mother. I'd give anything to hear her say, 'I love you.'"

Thelma began to think the whole world was against her. She grew depressed and bitter. Her life did not reflect the peace and joy of Christ. We asked her what was wrong. After a long silence and many tears she said, "Why didn't God give me a mother who loved me? Why didn't He control my cousins and uncle so they wouldn't abuse me?"

And then, as though all hope in life was gone, Thelma asked, "How can I trust God to control my life if He can't control these things?"

We shared that God allowed people free choice. When they chose to sin, He was more grieved than she was. That was why He had sent Jesus, to carry her griefs and sorrows. And that was why He had sent us, to show her His love. Suddenly it clicked. Thelma believed she could trust God and was sure that He loved her.

The long process of healing had begun.

THE GHETTO NEEDS A KING TO PROCLAIM JUSTICE FOR THE OPPRESSED

Justice and righteousness are synonymous. With Jesus, justice was not an ideal. It was a way of life.

If ever a person was treated unjustly it was Calvin. When Calvin was eight his mother divorced his father because he brutally beat her for no reason. Calvin and his eight brothers and sisters were split up and sent to different homes.

Calvin remembers, "It was hard making it without my father. He'd come by and say, 'Calvin, you're gonna be nobody. You're gonna fail. You're gonna wind up in jail.'"

That devastated Calvin. He told his father, "I'm your son, no matter what."

But his father responded, "Calvin, I don't know you no more than I know that tree standing there. You're a stranger to me. I don't wanna get to know you."

Calvin couldn't believe it. He prayed and prayed that God would restore his relationship with his father. He decided to try to reconcile one more time. So he walked up to his father's house and knocked on the door. Hesitantly he said, "Dad, I'd like to talk to you."

Calvin's father responded, "I'd like you to meet my son," pointing to a young man about Calvin's age. He continued, "I don't need you any more, Calvin. He's taken your place."

Calvin started to protest, but quickly abandoned hope.

His head drooped, his shoulders sagged. Tears streamed down his face. There is no justice in rejection.

Years before we had led Calvin to Christ. And now in the name of the One who brought justice to the poor we stood with Calvin.

Calvin told me, "I can't imagine where I would be today if I hadn't followed Christ. I'd probably be strung out on drugs, or maybe a teenage father with nothing to do. My life would have been wasted. But Jesus took all the hurt I had. He showed me how to forgive my father. Instead of bitterness, Jesus gave me love."

Jesus is performing His priestly, prophetic and kingly work through the missionaries of World Impact. We stand in awe of His sovereign power as He provides a crown of beauty instead of ashes, the oil of gladness instead of mourning and a garment of praise instead of a spirit of despair. He brings hope, healing and justice.

Tanisha, Thelma and Calvin are becoming "oaks of righteousness." They are recipients of redemption. Through the righteousness of God they have acquired life, beauty and utility, like an oak. They have new life—their weaknesses are being transformed into strength and durability. They have new beauty—the ugliness of sin is being replaced by the loveliness of Christ. And they are useful— their broken lives now display the splendor of the Lord.

It is through people like Tanisha, Thelma and Calvin that the cities will be renewed. These disciples are committed to staying in the ghetto as lights shining on a hill. They will bring hope and will draw others to Christ. They will provide the needed support, encouragement and models, so that the oppressed in our cities will no longer look at things as they are and ask "Why?" but will dream things as they should be, and ask, "Why not?"*

*Shaw, George Bernard, *Back to Methuselah* (paraphrase).

ONE FINAL WORD

World Impact is a Christian missions organization dedicated to bringing God's love to the ghettos of America. We develop indigenous disciples of Christ in the inner city by ministering to children, teenagers and adults who are committed to knowing Christ and to making Him known. They worship in culturally-conducive bodies that seek to honor and glorify God.

Transforming the hurt, oppression and devastation of the ghetto demands a long-term commitment by God's people. The Lord has given us highly dedicated, capable missionaries who live and minister in several major American ghettos including Newark, St. Louis, Wichita, Portland, Fresno, Los Angeles and San Diego. But they cannot minister effectively without your help.

There are many practical ways in which you can join us in bringing God's love to America's inner cities.

Be informed and pray

If you want to know more about our ministry in order to pray more specifically, you may:

• Receive World Impact's monthly *Bulletin*. Stories about our missionaries and the people to whom they minister update you on our outreach. Address your request to receive our *Bulletin* to our office.

If you wish to pray for a specific missionary please indicate this. You will receive his/her biographical sketch, address and phone number. Every month your missionary's prayer letter will be enclosed with our *Bulletin*.

• Read *They Dare to Love the Ghetto* (Regal Books, Ventura, CA, 1975, $1.95) by Keith Phillips. This modern-day missionary story traces the beginning of World Impact and shares God's marvelous intervention in the lives of hurting people.

• Read *The Making of a Disciple* (Fleming H. Revell Company, Old Tappan, NJ, 1981, $7.95 hardbound; $2.50 paperback) by Keith Phillips. This biblical statement on nurturing new believers to maturity in Christ explains World Impact's philosophy and strategy.

Give

Jesus said, "Where your treasure is, there your heart will be also" (Matt. 6:21). If you want to tangibly express your concern for brothers and sisters in need you may:

• Sponsor a child in one of our Bible clubs for $30 a year.

• Sponsor a Christian elementary school student for $25 a month.

• Contribute to our "Emergency Needs" fund to provide clothing, food, shelter or heating oil in Christ's name.

• Support a World Impact missionary. You will receive his/her monthly prayer letter.

• Give canned food, good used clothing, furniture, appliances, vehicles or other usable items to assist needy people. Write our office for the address of our ministry closest to you.

Come

Every week we have to turn away hundreds of children, teenagers and adults who want to know Christ and study His Word because we do not have enough missionaries to teach them. We need single adults, married couples—people from all walks of life, who want to minister to the poor by preaching and living the gospel in urban America. You may:

• Request a staff application from our office. We need Bible teachers, school teachers, vocational training teachers and businessmen. All of our staff members are full-time missionaries.

• Volunteer as a teacher's aide in one of our schools.

• Volunteer to repair cars, houses or other facilities.

• Lend your expertise and time in starting up and/or running a business to employ inner-city teenagers.

Inform Others

The best way for others to become acquainted with World Impact is for you to tell a friend. Distribute our *Bulletins*, suggest that people read our books, request a missionary speaker for your church or show one of our films in your church. Three excellent 16mm films are available to your church upon request from our office.

• *The Forgotten City* vividly describes World Impact's ministry of compassion (28 min.).

• *When Hell Freezes Over* graphically shows the blighted condition of the ghetto in winter. It speaks of human tragedy and an appropriate Christian response (20 min.).

• *Why Bother?* traces the lives of four Bible club children through adulthood. Two are living for Christ. One is a prostitute. One is in jail (20 min.).

For further information on becoming involved in bringing God's love to the ghettos of America, please write or call:

WORLD IMPACT
2001 S. Vermont Ave.
Los Angeles, CA 90007
(213) 735-1137